'Anyone interested in autism will treasure this book. McMahon-Coleman and Draisma have created a much-needed resource, which covers everything one needs to know about university students on the spectrum. A must-have for students on the spectrum, their families, as well as education professionals at all levels.'

*– Iva Strnadová, Associate Professor, University of New South Wales, Australia*

'McMahon-Coleman and Draisma have provided the higher education sector with a much-needed resource in a well-structured, easy-to-read guide to the provision of educational services to students with ASD. Grounded in their vast personal and professional experience, the deep insights within this book provide high-value reading for all those focussed on the teaching and learning of students with ASD.'

*– Dr Nola Norris, Morling College, Australia*

T0373020

Teaching University Students with
Autism Spectrum Disorder

# Teaching University Students with Autism Spectrum Disorder

## A Guide to Developing Academic Capacity and Proficiency

Kimberley McMahon-Coleman and Kim Draisma

Jessica Kingsley *Publishers*
London and Philadelphia

First published in 2016
by Jessica Kingsley Publishers
73 Collier Street
London N1 9BE, UK
and
400 Market Street, Suite 400
Philadelphia, PA 19106, USA

*www.jkp.com*

**Library of Congress Cataloging in Publication Data**
Names: McMahon-Coleman, Kimberley, author. | Draisma, Kim, author.
Title: Teaching university students with autism spectrum disorder : a guide
    to developing academic capacity and proficiency / Kimberley
    McMahon-Coleman and Kim Draisma.
Description: London ; Philadelphia : Jessica Kingsley Publishers, 2016. |
    Includes bibliographical references and index.
Identifiers: LCCN 2015050738 | ISBN 9781849054201 (alk. paper)
Subjects: LCSH: Autism spectrum disorders--Patients--Education (Higher) |
    Autistic people--Education (Higher)
Classification: LCC LC4717.5 .M46 2016 | DDC 378.0087--dc23
LC record available at http://lccn.loc.gov/2015050738

**British Library Cataloguing in Publication Data**
A CIP catalogue record for this book is available from the British Library

ISBN 978 1 84905 420 1
eISBN 978 0 85700 798 8

Printed and bound in Great Britain

*Dedicated to our students on the spectrum: past, present and future.*

# Contents

# Acknowledgements

In a longer-term project such as this, there are inevitably people whose support and encouragement make an enormous difference. We wish to acknowledge the many university students with Autism Spectrum Disorders who have enriched our teaching practice, but more specifically, those whose stories have been included in this book. You have helped us to assist the learning of countless others. Thank you to our University of Wollongong colleagues in Learning Development, Student Support Services and the faculties, but most particularly, our friends and colleagues in Disability Services, with whom we closely collaborate for the benefit of our students. A special shout-out to Petria McGoldrick, who proofread a late draft with incomparable enthusiasm. Our thanks must also be extended to Dr Nola Norris, whose thesis inspired us to look at some different ideas about autism, which is, of course, exactly what theses are supposed to do.

Thank you to my family: Rin, Luke, Imogen, Ben and Josipa Draisma, who enrich my life and support my projects. Thank you for your contributions, for fixing the computer and the wi-fi — and for making food and countless cups of tea; you kept me going. Thank you to Kimberley, who kept me on task when I really did not want to be, and who finished my sentences when I could not. As the final commitment in my academic career, this book is my small way of leaving a legacy.

*KD*

Thank you to Tony, Jamie and Robert Coleman, who have once again been supportive of a wife and mother whose head is sometimes elsewhere, but who enthusiastically celebrate our writing milestones all the same. And to Ellyn and David, Grace and Yeovanny, Dany, Viviana and Sofia; the Kajii, Hirose and Taguchi families; my wonderful godsons Jackson and Charlie and their mum Jody; Jo Evans and the little Js three; Phoebe Zeller and Nick and Alex Hawley; the Draisma clan and the inimitable Dr Roslyn Weaver: aren't I lucky to have the most wonderfully diverse and supportive extended adoptive family ever?

Some of the pages in this book began life as assignments in the Master of Education (Special Education) programme at the University of New South Wales. Special thanks to my classmates and to my very gifted lecturers – Associate Professor Iva Strnadova, Dr Therese M. (Terry) Cumming, Dr Sue O'Neill, and Lucy Kaan – who have all been an inspiration.

And to Kim: I really would have stopped at an article if it weren't for you.

*KMC*

Note: the names and some details of the individuals featured in this book have been changed, to protect their privacy.

# Preface

This book grew out of a number of conversations in our professional practice. We were both working in Learning Development, an academic language and learning unit that aims to assist students to develop their academic reading and writing skills. At the time, the unit had more than 20 academic staff and was operating across seven campuses, servicing a diverse range of undergraduate and postgraduate students, enrolled in any degree programme offered by the University. For many years, students whose learning needs were made more complex because of disability were typically seen by Kim. Eventually, it became apparent that this cohort was growing in both number and intensity, and an extra position was created and filled by Kimberley. The number of students with disabilities enrolling has continued to increase every year since, with students with Autism Spectrum Disorder (ASD) being one of the largest sub-cohorts. As we worked with the students and heard their stories, we began to realise how many of them were unware of conventions around study and behaviour within the higher education environment, and how many were struggling to meet the requirements of assessment. Our suspicions were confirmed repeatedly by teaching staff and the students who shared their classrooms. It became apparent, therefore, that there was a need for a book such as this to help the tertiary classroom practitioner who may not have an understanding or experience of Autism Spectrum Disorder.

We each have significant experience of Autism Spectrum Disorder, through both our professional and personal lives. While still a teenager Kim met the love of her life, who also happens to be on the high-functioning end of the spectrum, as is his identical twin, both of whom were university educated and held highly regarded professional positions before retirement. In the ensuing decades, therefore, she has spent a great deal of time socialising with family members on the spectrum, and she developed great understanding of how they interpreted and functioned within a neurotypical world. In her professional role as a secondary school teacher and later as an academic, Kim brought this considerable insight to her support of students with Autism Spectrum Disorder. She developed a professional reputation for assisting academic staff in the faculties to develop strategies to more effectively teach those same students. This culminated in Kim being invited to supervise a PhD student, whose research focused on talented adults with Autism Spectrum Disorder. That PhD was awarded in 2014.

Kimberley also began her professional life as a school teacher, and, despite doing very well in the 'Learners with Special Needs' subject during the Graduate Diploma of Education, had no idea what Asperger's Syndrome or the Autism Spectrum were when, as a beginning teacher, she was told that two of the 14 students in her Year 9 elective language class had been diagnosed with Asperger's. When she had children, the younger one resisted affection and took much longer to develop speech than his older sibling. By the time he was seven, she had befriended a number of people (via the internet) who were on the spectrum or parents of children on the spectrum. During a visit, one of these friends declared that she thought Kimberley's son was 'part of the tribe'. By this time, a first cousin had an Autism Spectrum Disorder diagnosis. At a session for Asperger Syndrome Partner Information Australia (ASPIA), clinical psychologist and well-known specialist in the field of Asperger's Syndrome, Tony Attwood, talked about the typical 'Aspie' family tree being evenly split between outgoing, gregarious types and socially awkward, introverted folks on the spectrum, which was certainly the case in Kimberley's family. In fact, Kimberley identified so strongly with much of what Attwood had to say, that the friend suggested she might benefit from an 'official' diagnosis! A few years later, the younger child announced that he had Googled 'that Asperger's Syndrome thing' and had 'almost all the symptoms'. At this point neither mother nor son has pursued an official diagnosis, as the workarounds employed seem to be working adequately to continue competently at work and in school.

We believe that our varied personal and professional experiences offer a depth of understanding that will prove useful to our tertiary teaching colleagues. If you would like to join our conversation, please continue via our blog: https://wordpress.com/design/ autismspectrumdisorderinhighereducation.wordpress.com or drop Kimberley a line via Twitter @KMcMahonColeman.

# Chapter 1

# Introducing the University Student on the Spectrum

*For many high-functioning individuals on the autism spectrum, college can be about as close as you can get to Heaven on Earth.*

(PERNER, 2002A)

In this introductory chapter we outline what the Autism Spectrum is and how students with autism may present. An increasing number of students are being diagnosed with Autism Spectrum Disorder (ASD), and a number of those who have been diagnosed as having 'Asperger's Syndrome' (as it is commonly termed, even though the official title is Asperger's Disorder) or 'High Functioning Autism' are now enrolling in post-secondary education. Tertiary educators therefore need to develop a range of teaching and communication strategies for this cohort. Our views have been developed through decades of work with students, family members, and friends on the spectrum and this book draws, most particularly, on our experiences as university teachers who have responsibility for assisting students with Autism Spectrum Disorder to achieve their potential in tertiary education.

Autism Spectrum Disorder is, as the name implies, a spectrum or continuum of disorders. These disorders are neurodevelopmental in nature and specifically affect development in the areas of social interaction, communication and behaviour (Adreon and Durocher, 2007). Autism Spectrum Disorder is defined in the *Diagnostic and Statistical Manual of Mental Disorders-5* as '[p]ersistent deficits in social communication and social interaction across multiple contexts' (American Psychiatric Association, 2013, p. 50). People at the higher functioning end of the spectrum are typified by an egocentric interest in a specific topic (Attwood, 2007) and average or above-average intellect (Dente and Parkinson, 2012), often demonstrating above-average attention to detail (Wolf, Thierfeld Brown and Kukiela Bork, 2009). All of these features make students on the spectrum excellent candidates for tertiary study (Bolick, 2006).

However, impairments in communication can impact on both the social and educational aspects of schooling and tertiary learning. As Jill Locke, Connie Kasari and Jeffrey Wood argue, students on the spectrum experience challenges around social pragmatics, such as taking conversational turns, initiating conversations and understanding or having empathy for the listener's perspective, engaging in perseverative speech and showing inappropriate emotional regulation and expression (Locke, Kasari and Wood, 2014; Murza and Nye, 2013). This is critical in the higher education context, where much of the teaching is transmitted in auditory mode via mass lectures, seminars and tutorial discussions. Issues in these areas can also impact on social functioning and peer relationships, which, in turn, can cause problems with learning and teaching if students respond inappropriately during teacher-led classwork or within student-participatory groupwork in tutorials or practical classes.

Because autism represents a spectrum of behaviours, two individuals on the spectrum might behave quite differently (Bradshaw, 2013). As Diane Adreon and Jennifer Durocher note, symptoms 'can occur in any combination and can range from very mild to very severe' (Adreon and Durocher, 2007, p. 272). Indeed, controversies over the differences between high-functioning autism,

Asperger's syndrome, and Pervasive Developmental Disorder not otherwise specified (PDD-NOS) have led, in part, to the significant diagnostic changes between the fourth and fifth versions of the *Diagnostic and Statistical Manual of Mental Disorders.*

Lorna Wing identified a triad of areas where delays might be viewed in an autistic individual: social interaction, social communication and social behaviour (Yoshida, 2012). Known as Asperger's Syndrome, this presentation was identified as a separate disorder on the spectrum with the 1994 publication of the Fourth Edition of the *Diagnostic and Statistical Manual of Mental Disorders,* commonly known as the *DSM-IV* (American Psychiatric Association, 2000). The manual cites the essential features of Asperger's Disorder as being: a severe and sustained impairment in social interaction; the development of restricted, repetitive patterns of behaviour, interests and activities; and clinical impairment of social, occupational or other important areas of functioning (American Psychiatric Association, 2000). It cites a further two criteria, one of which is predicated on its difference to autism: '[in] contrast to Autistic Disorder, there are no clinically significant delays or deviance in language acquisition' (American Psychiatric Association, 2000, p. 80), noting that some of the 'more subtle aspects' of social communication, such as give-and-take in conversation, may be noticeably deficient. The definition of Asperger's Disorder was also marked by an absence of delays in the acquisition of age-appropriate learning skills, adaptive behaviours and intellectual disability (American Psychiatric Association, 2000). The section on differential diagnosis points out that while both disorders involved abnormality in terms of social interaction, in Asperger's Disorder, restricted and repetitive interests manifest as an all-encompassing pursuit of a particular interest, rather than the process of a motor mannerism (or 'stim') or preoccupations with objects or rituals (American Psychiatric Association, 2000). Social interaction patterns are characterised as being marked by social isolation in autism, as opposed to eccentric, verbose and insensitive social interaction in individuals with Asperger's

Syndrome (American Psychiatric Association, 2000). The *DSM-IV* listed six areas of potential difficulty that governed diagnosis: severe and sustained impairment in social interaction; restricted, repetitive patterns of behaviour, interests and activities; clinically significant impairment in social, occupational or other important areas of functioning; no clinically significant language delays or cognitive development; and not meeting the criteria for Pervasive Developmental Disorder or schizophrenia (American Psychiatric Association, 2000).

Further, the prognosis for Asperger's was noted as being 'significantly better than in Autistic Disorder, as follow-up studies suggest that, as adults, many individuals are capable of gainful employment and personal self-sufficiency' (American Psychiatric Association, 2000, p. 82). It is perhaps no surprise, then, that among the cohort enrolling in tertiary studies, those who identified as having Asperger's Syndrome were more prevalent than those who identified as having autism; after all, a certain level of 'personal self-sufficiency' is required to complete a Bachelor's degree or higher. The authors of Kaplan and Sadock's *Synopsis of Psychiatry* concur, noting that a good prognosis is associated with a normal IQ and high-level social skills, even though the individual may still relate to others awkwardly, appear socially uncomfortable and display unusual thought patterns (Sadock and Sadock, 2007), and that some capacity for identifying 'self-sufficiency and problem-solving techniques' is helpful in social and work settings (Sadock and Sadock, 2007, p. 1202).

Somewhat controversially, Asperger's Syndrome as a distinct diagnosis was removed from the Fifth Edition of the *Diagnostic and Statistical Manual of Mental Disorders* (*DSM-5*), published in May 2013. Instead, this latest version of the manual includes Asperger's Disorder under the diagnosis of 'Autism Spectrum Disorder' (ASD):

> Individuals with a well-established *DSM-IV* diagnosis of autistic disorder, Asperger's disorder, or Pervasive Developmental Disorder not otherwise specified should be

given the diagnosis of **Autism Spectrum Disorder**. (American Psychiatric Association, 2013, p. 51, emphasis added)

The diagnostic criteria for Autism Spectrum Disorder contained in the *DSM-5* include the criteria previously used to describe Asperger's Disorder in the *DSM-IV*, most notably placing the focus on deficits in social communication and interaction.

**Table 1.1: Comparison of DSM-IV and DSM-5 broad diagnostic criteria**

| Asperger's Disorder (DSM-IV) (See American Psychiatric Association, 2000, p. 80) | Autism Spectrum Disorder (DSM-5) (See American Psychiatric Association, 2013, pp. 50–51) |
|---|---|
| Severe and sustained impairment in social interaction | Persistent deficits in social communication and social interaction across multiple contexts |
| Restricted, repetitive patterns of behaviour, interests and activities | Restricted, repetitive patterns of behaviour, interests or activities |
| Clinically significant impairment in social, occupational or other important areas of functioning | Clinically significant impairment in social, occupational or other important areas of functioning |
| No clinically significant language delays or cognitive development | Must be present in early developmental period |
| Criteria not met for Pervasive Developmental Disorder or schizophrenia | May co-occur with intellectual disability. Not better explained by intellectual disability or global developmental delay |

The *DSM-5* provides detailed examples related to each of its broad criteria to assist in diagnosis (see American Psychiatric Association, 2013, pp. 50–51). Further, the *DSM-5* tabulates the severity of the disorder from Level 3 down to Level 1. Those in Level 1 are high-functioning individuals requiring some support (as opposed to requiring substantial or very substantial support), with no diagnosis of intellectual disability (American Psychiatric Association, 2013; Yoshida, 2012). This category includes the individuals formerly identified as having Asperger's, who may, in fact, have very advanced intelligence and academic ability (Wolf, Thierfeld Brown and Kukiela Bork, 2009). Because of the social requirements of educational settings, however, the transition to tertiary study may still pose significant issues, regardless of innate ability or even aptitude for a particular field of study. Best-practice strategies that we, as tertiary teachers, can use to accommodate these issues are the focus of this book. It is important to note, however, that students on the spectrum will fall along a continuum of learner differences (Healey, Bradley, Fuller and Hall, 2006) and therefore there can be no one-size-fits-all method to assist with their learning. While we do make some generalisations about types of behaviour that this cohort might display in a classroom and make suggestions about how to respond, ultimately what is required is a person-centred approach that takes into consideration the strengths and challenges of the individual, based on sound pedagogical strategies.

Predictably, since students on the spectrum are often resistant to change, students formerly known as having Asperger's are, in many cases, confused or even insulted by the change in nomenclature (Norris, 2014; Skuse, 2012), which dictates that educators may need to exercise some caution when discussing traits of the disorder in students. As a general rule, if a student discloses the nature of their condition, it is best to use that same term in future dealings. For those students who identify as having Asperger's Syndrome, this is the better term to use with the student, regardless of what the *DSM-5* might say or the terminology that you might use with other professionals. Conversely, if a student identifies as autistic, she or he may correct you if you use the term 'Asperger's'. Similarly, if a student has not disclosed an official diagnosis, it is far better to use phrases like 'for literal thinkers like yourself' when introducing the student to some effective study strategies. Minor 'corrections' have the capacity to become major distractions or philosophical debates about diagnosis and disability (especially if the individual's 'special interest' happens to be the nature of their disorder).

It is worth noting that women and girls on the spectrum may present somewhat differently. It was long thought that the incidence of Autism Spectrum Disorder was lower in girls, but it now seems more likely that they are better able to 'mask' their symptomatic behaviours, and, as Yuko Yoshida argues, 'there is growing recognition that if children with milder cases are included, the prevalence among girls is higher than previously thought' (Yoshida, 2012, p. 85). Rudy Simone argues in her book, *Aspergirls*, it is not so much that the symptoms are different, as that they may be perceived differently. While female students on the spectrum will have similar academic challenges to their male counterparts, they may not draw the attention of the teacher quite so readily (Freedman, 2010). For example, hyperlexia and early reading in girls may just be seen as signs of intelligence and it may be assumed that emotional intelligence and maturity are also ahead of the curve, even when they are not; as long as obsessions or special interests are in socially acceptable areas such as art, music or books, they may not be as noticeable as when a boy eschews sport for an interest in Monet or van Gogh (Simone, 2010). Tony Attwood suggests that teenage girls with Asperger's Syndrome display greater verbal capacity and fluency, which can manifest in a passion for literature and drama and highly developed writing skills. Because of their 'fascination with words [they may eventually] become successful authors, poets or academics in English literature' (Attwood, 2006, p. 6). Finally, there is some conjecture that girls may be better mimics than boys, and typically have different profiles of social and communication skills (Williams *et al.*, 2008).

## Autism Spectrum Disorder and higher education

With the prevalence of high-functioning autism apparently increasing (Adreon and Durocher, 2007; Dente and Parkinson, 2012; Dixon and Tanner, 2013), so too are the numbers of students on the spectrum enrolling in post-secondary education (Wenzel and Rowley, 2010). Described as a 'burgeoning population', the number of people with the diagnosis has also led to increased awareness of the disorder. The inclusive education movement comes from a philosophical base of providing for all children within the community, regardless of age, background or disability (Foreman and Arthur-Kelly, 2014). With the associated shift in special education over the past two decades, an increasing number of people with disabilities are completing high school and considering going on to post-compulsory education. In the spirit of assessing a student's attainments, skills and strengths (Foreman and Arthur-Kelly, 2014), people with disabilities are now encouraged to live as normal a life as possible, with valid social roles and participation in community events taking place in the least restrictive environment possible. For many young people, the social role of choice is that of student.

The 1994 Salamanca Statement (UNESCO, 1994) endorsed the idea that all children should be able to access a comprehensive education; that students should not be refused an education because they are perceived to be more difficult to teach. This idea has been entrenched in legislation in most developed countries. While the earlier UN Convention on the Rights of the Child stipulated that primary education should be compulsory and free, with access to secondary and tertiary education to be made accessible according to capacity (United Nations General Assembly, 1989), the Salamanca Statement goes further, arguing for 'equality of opportunity for children, youth and adults with disabilities in primary, secondary and tertiary education carried out, in so far as is possible, in integrated settings' (UNESCO, 1994, p. 17). These two governing documents have led, over time, to an increase in the number of students with disabilities completing secondary schooling and looking to enrol in tertiary and higher education alongside their peers. Within the cohort of students with disabilities, those on the Autism Spectrum 'typically present with intellectual and academic skills that make them excellent candidates for college' (Bolick, 2006, p. 82). They are among those most likely to be interested in a university qualification since they often have high intelligence and a specialised area of interest that they wish to pursue. Where once these students may have attended community or technical colleges or not attempted tertiary study at all (Martino McCarty,

2012; Wenzel and Rowley, 2010), it is now more likely that they will attempt to complete Bachelor degrees and subsequent higher degrees. Therefore, a greater understanding of the needs of those on the spectrum will lead to better educational accommodations and graduation outcomes.

Despite improvements in enrolment and attendance, however, the evidence suggests that significant changes could still be made: American studies suggest that only 12 per cent of students with disabilities graduate from college (Trent Bruce, 2014); a 2013 study by Autism Spectrum Australia (ASPECT) showed that only 13 per cent of surveyed Australians with autism held Bachelor degrees or higher; a statistic that is well below the 25 per cent level for all Australians reported by the Australian Bureau of Statistics in 2011 (ASPECT, 2013). In the United States, it is estimated that less than 2 per cent of the university population is on the spectrum (George Washington University School of Education and Human Development, n.d.). A 2010 Ontario-based report noted that although 5800 students on the spectrum would be completing high school within the next two years, less than a quarter had indicated that they intended to apply for entry to tertiary education – but that even that number represented a three-fold increase over the number already enrolled (Alcorn Mackay, 2010). A study in the United Kingdom also found exponential enrolment growth in this cohort: a 77 per cent increase, nationally, in the three years to 2010–11 (Hatswell, Harding, Martin and Baron-Cohen, 2013).

While there has been a significant increase in the number of students with disabilities enrolling in tertiary education, a significant proportion of these do not graduate (Garrison-Wade and Lehmann, 2009; George Washington University School of Education and Human Development, n.d.; Trent Bruce, 2014). *We Belong*, the first large-scale Australian study about the 'life experiences, aspirations and support needs of adults who have an Autism Spectrum Disorder (ASD) with no co-occurring intellectual disability' (ASPECT, 2013, p. 5) found similar results. Although 81 per cent of those surveyed had commenced a course of study at a vocational education provider such as a Technical and Further

Education (TAFE) institute, university or other accredited tertiary provider, 23 per cent also reported that they had abandoned that qualification. Most left because of concomitant mental health issues and/or unmet learning support needs (ASPECT, 2013). Clearly, higher education providers need to review policies and procedures until the outcomes of this cohort are more-or-less commensurate with those of the overall student population, particularly given the high level of intelligence typically found within this cohort (Trent Bruce, 2014; Wenzel and Rowley, 2010). There are few studies discussing university students with Autism Spectrum Disorder, so best practices for this cohort have not yet really been established within the literature (Martino McCarty, 2012; Trent Bruce, 2014). Further, data about retention, graduation and employment is unknown and warrants further research as a matter of some urgency (Trent Bruce, 2014). As ASPECT argues, what little research has been done serves only to 'indicate high levels of both perceived need, and unmet support for those needs' (ASPECT, 2013, p. 24). This book attempts to redress this to some extent by suggesting support strategies that we have developed and seen succeed.

Because autism is primarily a social disability, students on the spectrum are likely to require additional assistance in order to negotiate the social terrain and to comprehend and meet academic expectations. The transition to university is one that is difficult for neurotypical students, but even more so for students on the spectrum whose brains are often said to be 'wired differently' (Norris, 2014, p. 30) with deficits in Theory of Mind and central coherence (Wolf, Thierfeld Brown and Kukiela Bork, 2009). Issues in relation to social skills manifest not only in social situations, but also in the classroom as students are expected to navigate groupwork, group discussions and graded participation (Dente and Parkinson, 2012). University students are expected to be personally responsible and self-advocate (Adreon and Durocher, 2007; Dente and Parkinson, 2012), but students on the spectrum have impairments in understanding social situations, in initiating conversations, and in understanding *faux pas* (Attwood, 2007;

Wolf, Thierfeld Brown and Kukiela Bork, 2009), which makes it unlikely that such students will be well positioned to effectively seek assistance or advice. Indeed, they may not know that their understanding of an academic or social situation is inaccurate, or that they need help. Equally, students on the spectrum may be unusually social in that they have difficulty knowing when to stop talking in a lecture theatre or classroom, or knowing when to listen, or what to derive from aurally presented information or instructions. In some cases, they may become inappropriately dependent on a lecturer or tutor, using patterns of behaviour established with aides in primary or secondary school, unaware that the lecturer has other responsibilities than assisting that particular student. Some universities or colleges may appoint a student aide or mentor to assist (Suciu, 2014), but this, too, must be monitored in case of dependent relationships developing.

Apart from social interactions in the classroom, comprehension (Adreon and Durocher, 2007) and, in particular, verbal comprehension (ASPECT, 2013) is potentially an area of concern. Further, many students on the spectrum have 'significant deficit[s] in many aspects of executive functioning' (Adreon and Durocher, 2007, p. 276) and may find it difficult to manage long-term projects or establish and maintain study schedules (ASPECT, 2013). These individuals are likely to prefer routine, but workloads typically intensify as the semester goes on, rendering routines established early potentially less than adequate during prime assessment season. Assessments themselves may prove opaque and the instructions might require interpretation or clarification. Even if the question is understood, writing can create an increased cognitive load for students on the spectrum since writing is a communicative act that requires students to plan, generate, organise and revise text, all while maintaining a sense of audience (Pennington and Delano, 2012) and foregrounding assessment requirements.

It is, of course, no surprise when one considers the etymology of the word 'autism' that these students find it difficult to step outside of the self-focus. Some students with Autism Spectrum

Disorder experience sensitivity to sounds, aromas, textures and touch (Attwood, 2007), and these may prove impossible to manage in large lecture halls. Liane Holliday Willey recalls that because of her intelligence and abilities, 'there was no reason for anyone to suspect [she] needed special counselling or special tutoring or mentoring' (Holliday Willey, 1999, p. 48), but that she found the 'confusing, rambling, crowded and expansive campus' an 'assault' on her senses (Holliday Willey, 1999, p. 48). Finally, there is a high comorbidity of anxiety and depression with Autism Spectrum Disorders (vanBergeijk, Klin and Volkmar, 2008). As students age and are expected to engage in higher order cognitive processes, they often withdraw into themselves (Freedman, 2010) and became more aware of their social inadequacies (Sansosti and Powell-Smith, 2010). Anxiety and depression become even more problematic at exam time since even neurotypical students will experience some anxiety around testing and examinations, and those on the spectrum may have their anxiety further exacerbated by experiencing these events as changes to routine (vanBergeijk, Klin and Volkmar, 2008).

Despite all these possible challenges, the university or college experience is often rewarding for individuals on the spectrum; students describe tertiary education as a 'vast improvement over high school' (Wolf, Thierfeld Brown and Kukiela Bork, 2009, p. 232). Achieving a level of education commensurate with one's ability is an important step in self-actualisation (ASPECT, 2013; Martino McCarty, 2012). Many graduates with Autism Spectrum Disorder report enjoying the process of studying. Professor of Special Education and founder of the AutismAsperger.net site, Stephen Shore, has stated that he found university to be 'an exciting time' where he could be himself (Adreon and Durocher, 2007, p. 278). ASPECT found that the 'largely solitary nature of studying and learning may also hold special appeal' (ASPECT, 2013, p. 48), while still others suggested that university-aged students are likely to be more tolerant of individual differences, and that students on the spectrum may find neurotypical peers who share their interests studying in the same field (Wolf, Thierfeld Brown and Kukiela Bork, 2009). Universities and colleges can be safe havens for individuals with autism; after all, these institutions do provide an environment wherein an intense preoccupation with a favourite subject is actually encouraged (Ackerman, Gross, Heisely and Perner, 2005). As Wolf *et al.* argue, a 'dedicated and (occasionally) obsessive student can be mentored to become a diligent lab or research assistant' (Wolf, Thierfeld Brown and Kukiela Bork, 2009, p. 174).

In some cases, students will attain 'degrees and even doctorates' (Bradshaw, 2013, p. 47) because, after all, writing a doctoral thesis is 'a well-trodden path for intelligent people with good academic records who hold an interest in an obscure topic and are able to focus on it with unusual intensity for an extended period of time' (McMahon-Coleman, 2013, p. 11). Indeed, academic Lars Perner has argued that the academic environment is one in which 'eccentric people, at least within reason, are tolerated and sometimes even admired' (Perner, 2002b). Nobel Laureate Vernon Smith concurs, referring to the 'deficiencies and selective advantages' of autism, suggesting that his capacity for deep concentration and an ability to ignore professional pressure led to his Nobel prize (cited in Herera, 2005). Educator Sheila Wagner points out that the unusual sartorial and food choices, and compromised cooking and housekeeping practices to which students on the spectrum may be prone, may actually blend in better in the college environment than elsewhere (Wagner, 2002).

Despite these well-rehearsed arguments that university study is attainable and desirable for many students on the spectrum, there is surprisingly little research on the retention and graduation rates of students with Autism Spectrum Disorder. There are, however, a number of international studies that use qualitative responses and advice from people on the spectrum who have succeeded at university, and others that extrapolate established best secondary educational practice to the tertiary environment. These are further explored in Chapter 3.

## Planning for transition

Individuals do not have an inalienable right to tertiary education, but nor can they be denied one on the basis of a disability (Dell, Newton and Petroff, 2012). Students on the spectrum have often remained unidentified within the tertiary education system, even though they are likely to require additional assistance in order to negotiate the social terrain and to comprehend and meet academic expectations. Although in one sense universities and colleges may become safe havens for these students because there is a legitimate space to examine a special interest in detail, they also represent a new learning environment and a new set of social expectations. In order to have the opportunity to study a niche subject in close detail, students must first survive the transition to university – one that is difficult for neurotypical students, and more so for students on the spectrum. A number of experts agree that planning the transition to tertiary education must begin early in an attempt to mitigate the anxiety about change typically experienced by students on the spectrum (Dixon and Tanner, 2013; Eckes and Ochoa, 2005; Garrison-Wade and Lehmann, 2009; Strnadova and Cumming, 2016; vanBergeijk, Klin and Volkmar, 2008; Wenzel and Rowley, 2010).

Under the Americans with Disabilities Act (1990) and Individuals with Disabilities Act (IDEA) 2004, the UK's Equality Act (2011), and Australia's Disability Discrimination Act (1992) and Disability Standards for Education (2005), it is unlawful to discriminate against someone because of a disability, and reasonable adjustments must be made to accommodate disabilities (so long as they do not unduly disadvantage non-disabled students or the institution itself). The legislation is generally less prescriptive than it is for primary and secondary schools in recognition that not everyone goes on to higher education, but everyone deserves a basic education (UN General Assembly, 1989). For example, in the United States, every school student with a registered disability must have an individualised learning plan under IDEA; however, there is no correlating legislation within the higher education sector. How effectively students are supported in the tertiary environment relies more heavily on the goodwill of staff.

In Australia and a number of other countries, students with disabilities are offered certain educational protections under law (Australian Federal Government, 1992; Disability Standards for Education, 2005). The (Australian) Disability Standards for Education mean that reasonable adjustments must be made so that students with disabilities can enrol, access and participate in the curriculum; further, that they must have reasonable access to student support services and that institutions must work to eliminate harassment and victimisation (Disability Standards for Education, 2005). Indeed, higher education institutions are encouraged to develop equity plans that are then used to allocate federal government funding targeting widening participation (Newland, Boyd and Pavey, 2006). For this university access to happen and be recorded, however, the student with a disability must first assume primary responsibility for her or his disability and initiate all negotiations around accommodations, since colleges and universities have no legal responsibilities to identify students (Dell, Newton and Petroff, 2012). It may be difficult for some students to take on the role of self-advocate, particularly if their parents have acted as their advocates during compulsory schooling (Strnadova and Cumming, 2016). Accommodations are means of making the curriculum more accessible to students, such as raising the level of a desk so that a wheelchair can fit under it, or, most commonly, increased time in examinations or to submit assignments. All adjustments must be 'reasonable', but this term is not defined; instead, it is always open to debate (Dell, Newton and Petroff, 2012). Unlike modifications, accommodations do not necessitate changing the nature of the task, but rather, the means by which the task is completed. Students, disability services professionals and academic faculty must agree on which accommodations are necessary and 'reasonable'; any accommodations that faculty academics argue detract from the key learning outcomes will not be granted. For example, excusing a student with a social phobia from a practicum experience may detract from the core learning outcomes and experiences of the course and would thus be modifying the course, as opposed to accommodating the disability of the student. Prior to any of this negotiation, however, the student must first disclose to the institution that they have a disability, and its nature, and initiate discussions with appropriate support services. This is, of course, rather a difficult process for those with a social disability such as Autism Spectrum Disorder.

Anecdotal evidence, including conversations with students themselves and attempts by colleagues to collate data about the number of students with disabilities, supports research that suggests that disclosure levels may not be representative of the true number of students with disabilities enrolling (Adams and Brown, 2006). There is, typically, little to no dialogue between secondary schools and universities prior to enrolment, even though the literature shows that all transition planning should begin well ahead of the transition and include effective communication between all stakeholders (Strnadova and Cumming, 2016). Part of the issue, here, of course, is that family involvement is not usually expected in post-secondary environments (Dell, Newton and Petroff, 2012); nor is it really welcomed, given that students are considered adults over the age of 18 years and entitled to the provisions of privacy legislation. Any negotiations that do take place are likely to only involve a meeting with Disability Support Service personnel, rather than faculty academics and/or other support units, such as writing centres or learning development centres. Greater interaction between educational settings (high school to college or university) would help establish the kinds of supports a particular individual needs or has become used to, enabling better service to students (Eckes and Ochoa, 2005) and for negotiations about future adjustments to be made prior to the commencement of the first semester of study. Adreon and Durocher lament the lack of focus that has been placed on the transition process for this cohort, noting that the proportion of students on the spectrum attending post-secondary education is only likely to increase over time (Adreon and Durocher, 2007), thanks to trends towards earlier and more effective diagnosis and intervention (vanBergeijk, Klin and Volkmar, 2008). The differences between secondary and tertiary education can be overwhelming if a student is not prepared (Strnadova and Cumming, 2016); equally, it can be confronting for teaching staff with no personal experience with this cohort to manage the more unusual quirks of behaviour. It is important to be aware of the potential negative impacts of acting on stigma or stereotypes, and instead focus on the teaching of the students. Indeed, the good practice principles outlined in this book will benefit *all* students (Hall and Stahl, 2006; Stanovich and Jordan, 2000).

## Supports that work

There are a number of supports that, in our experience, work to assist students to succeed at university: social accommodations, logistical accommodations and academic accommodations.

### Social accommodations

A number of social skills may need to be explicitly explained and taught in order for students on the spectrum to fully participate in a range of university classrooms. Drawing on the work of Glennon (2001), Gordon and others (2002) and vanBergeijk and colleagues (vanBergeijk, Klin and Volkmar, 2008), Marguerite Martino McCarty recommended the use of intentional social accommodations such as peer mentoring and social skills training (Martino McCarty, 2012). While social skills training is certainly key and some instances of subject mentoring that we have observed appear to work very well, Natalie Trent Bruce sounds a note of caution, citing other studies that voice concern that peer help necessitates disclosure of disability to a potential classmate. She further argues that the quality and accuracy of assistance from a peer may be lacking when compared with that offered by a more qualified teaching assistant, professional staff member or academic (Trent Bruce, 2014). While the question of who should offer support is worthy of debate, what does seem clear is that discussing possible scenarios for managing groupwork and group assignments is beneficial for students on the spectrum, who find them to be anxiety-inducing exercises otherwise. The University of Connecticut offers a non-credit bearing course for students with Autism Spectrum Disorder that teaches skills such as taking turns in class, listening skills and respectful classroom behaviour (Wenzel and Rowley, 2010). While this seems useful, it should be noted that this is a targeted transition programme for students on the spectrum and comes at an additional cost. The authors are not aware of any such programme in Australia or the United Kingdom. It would seem, therefore, that a more useful strategy is to assist faculty staff to more effectively teach students with Autism Spectrum Disorder. In making teaching and assessment transparent, explicit and unambiguous, all students – including those on the spectrum – are more likely to meet course outcomes.

It is important to note that not all students with Autism Spectrum Disorder will have made contact with the university's Disability Unit, or disclosed their condition to teaching staff. Indeed, some students may even be undiagnosed or not recognise that they behave differently to others. Yet, it is likely that all students on the spectrum will find challenges within the changes to routine, altered expectations and hidden curriculum that are inherent in transitioning to the tertiary environment. It is not the role of the tertiary educator to diagnose or label students, but a working knowledge of certain behaviours that might be symptomatic of the syndrome will assist the teacher in deciding more useful inclusive classroom strategies when particular behavioural quirks are apparent in individual students. All good teaching is predicated on establishing highly effective working relationships and trust between teacher and students; this is a task that will require special care when a student has a social disability, such as Autism Spectrum Disorder.

## *Logistical accommodations*

Numerous publications on matriculating with Autism Spectrum Disorder recommend becoming familiar with the campus before starting studies (Adreon and Durocher, 2007; Harpur, Lawlor and Fitzgerald, 2004; Holliday Willey, 1999). This is a particularly useful strategy for this cohort, for, as Dawn Prince-Hughes argues, the social demands and physical environment of university or college campuses may be 'at odds with the innate needs and motivations of college students with A[utism] S[pectrum] D[isorder]' (cited in Adreon and Durocher, 2007, p. 278). To overcome this, some tertiary institutions provide student mentors to guide students on the spectrum around the campus for an orientation period in semester 1, including travelling with them from one class to another in order to establish familiarity with the physical environment. Students may also need to adjust their expectations around routines, timetables and schedules, since these tend to be less rigid in the tertiary learning environment than they are in high schools (Strnadova and Cumming, 2016).

A 12-year longitudinal study of students with disabilities in Canada found that students who undertook lighter workloads earned the same grades and attained the same graduation rates as students without disabilities (Trent Bruce, 2014). A reduced study load is one of the more common recommendations made for students with disabilities; within the Australian context, however, this has significant financial implications as a part-time load disqualifies a student from eligibility for Austudy, which is government-funded fortnightly income to undertake the degree. Other ways of modifying the study load are discussed in Chapters 3, 4 and 5.

Preferred timetables are a commonly recommended reasonable adjustment. This allows students to think about the times when they are likely to be most alert and the times when they are likely to be in sensorial overload, and to schedule classes accordingly, where possible. Adreon and Durocher go so far as to advise scheduling classes only one or two days per week in the first semester of study (Adreon and Durocher, 2007), mindful that this necessitates a reduced study load. A preferred timetable allows an individual student to think about her or his own learning needs and to attempt to create a timetable more likely to facilitate than hinder success.

Other logistical accommodations commonly occur around examination time, allowing students on the spectrum extra time for cognitive processing, or individual or small-room exams to minimise sensory overload.

## Academic accommodations

Although academeic considerations are discussed in greater depth in the following chapters, it is important to mention them here, in a general sense. As previously mentioned, students on the spectrum may have issues in the field of executive function. These can manifest in the areas of planning, note-taking, study skills, memory strategies, organisational skills, self-monitoring and timetabling (Strnadova and Cumming, 2016), all of which are discussed in more detail in Chapter 4. The coping strategies that worked across year-long subjects in high school may not translate well to 13-week semester blocks. As Christine Wenzel and Laura Rowley note, all first-year students are likely to need to re-learn academic strategies that suit the tertiary setting; for students who find change difficult, such as those on the spectrum, however, explicit teaching of new strategies may be needed in order to reduce stress (Wenzel and Rowley, 2010). The use of low-tech assistive organisational tools, such as wall planners and student diaries (provided free of charge at some institutions), are a good starting point, but the student may require explicit teaching of how best to utilise these resources. These are further explored in Chapter 5.

Given that students on the spectrum are prone to very literal interpretations (Adreon and Durocher, 2007), they may find assessment instructions particularly opaque. Well-meaning attempts to use metaphor or offer additional guidelines in the form of marking rubrics may only add to the cognitive load. Further, in our experience, feedback can sometimes cause confusion. Much of the tertiary curriculum remains hidden; beginning students who are first in family, very literal and have no particular awareness of how university systems work may be very upset to receive a 'D' grade, unaware that a 'D' at university represents a Distinction, when in high school it represented working below year level. Teachers need to make explicit these opaque or implicit codes, as we will see in Chapter 3.

Any student transitioning to university or college is likely to feel intimidated and dislocated (Harpur, Lawlor and Fitzgerald, 2004; Perner, 2002b). For students with what is essentially a social disability, the transition may be one fraught with anxiety. As Stephen Bradshaw argues, the education system as a whole may seem 'unwelcoming at best and a complete nightmare and totally inappropriate at worst for anyone with a difficulty in social communication' (Bradshaw, 2013, p. 156). The tertiary learning environment is a complex one wherein students might have to manage quite disparate expectations. As we have noted, there are some significant appeals to a degree programme, but these will also likely propose significant challenges. Nuanced differences between class types – such as tutorials, workshops, seminars, laboratories and lectures – mean that students must show a certain amount of adaptability when thinking about expected classroom behaviours. Students may well be expected to participate in tutorial or workshop discussions, for example, but are often actively discouraged from interrupting an otherwise monodirectional lecture. When time is provided for students to ask questions at the end of a lecture, they may misinterpret this invitation or be unable to hold their question in mind until the end and, instead, interrupt throughout the presentation. Similarly, on the assessment front, a student who has mastered a book report might then not grasp the differences inherent in a tutorial paper; or, having mastered essay writing, might suddenly be faced with a structured report. Students undertaking interdisciplinary studies may face an increased layer of complexity as they juggle competing expectations and referencing styles.

## Conclusion

We have identified several broad areas that may represent stumbling blocks for students on the spectrum. In the following chapters we address discipline matches and mismatches; interpreting expectations and codes of conduct; issues with overly rigid and literal thinking; dealing with project planning and multi-tasking; self-monitoring and central coherence. Not all students will exhibit all of the behaviours identified by the *DSM-5* and not all will experience difficulties with the issues listed here. By arranging the discussion in this way, however, it should make it easier for a tertiary teacher to find information that is useful, while juggling the myriad teaching responsibilities that occur each semester. Each chapter features at least one case study to examine how this can and does play out in a tertiary classroom environment. Strategies for classroom practitioners are then explored, followed by how they worked in the particular case study. We are mindful that, unlike their school-based peers, not all teachers in a university or college have undertaken formal teacher training. As an appendix to each chapter, key 'Tips for Teachers' and 'Tips for Learners' are included as a quick tool for those seeking immediate ideas.

We hope this practical approach will offer some useful 'take home' advice and strategies for understanding the cultural chasm that can sometimes form when students with unusual and often rigid learning characteristics meet the potentially equally rigid expectations of tertiary education.

# Chapter 2

# Discipline Matches and Mismatches

## University disciplines

University or college 'disciplines' are well-established branches of knowledge or fields of learning that embody a system of tacit rules of conduct. Universities and colleges are normally organised into 'faculties' that identify as a particular discipline for administrative purposes and for the organisation of teaching and research that leads to publication. Although there are no formal criteria that define academic disciplines and sub-disciplines, nor is there international or even national agreement on the classification of fields of study within a particular discipline, there nevertheless exist common understandings between academics and between universities about what, notionally, constitutes a discipline. Discipline boundaries typically settle on: Humanities (Arts, Creative and Fine Arts, History, Literature, Linguistics, Philosophy, Religion); Social Sciences (Anthropology, Archaeology, Cultural Studies, Education, Economics, Human Geography, Politics or Political Science, Psychology, Sociology); Natural Sciences (Biology, Chemistry, Physics, Physical Geography or Earth Sciences, Space Sciences, Sport or Exercise Sciences); Mathematical

Sciences (Pure and Applied Mathematics, Statistics, Logic, Computer Sciences); and professional faculties that mostly focus on one profession, such as Medicine, Nursing, Physiotherapy, Pathology, Pharmacy, Engineering (Computer, Electrical, Materials, Mechanical, Structural Engineering), Business or Commerce (including Accountancy, Management, Marketing, Economics), Law, Journalism and others. Foucault likened the disciplines to the prison system: '[t]he disciplines characteri[s]e, classify, speciali[s]e; they distribute along a scale, around a norm, hierarchi[s]e individuals in relation to one another and, if necessary, disqualify and invalidate' (Foucault, 1977, p. 223).

When students enrol in a university degree course, they will be educated in a particular discipline or body of knowledge, such as English Literature, that is itself sub-divided into subjects, such as Medieval Drama, Shakespeare and his Contemporaries, Eighteenth Century Prose, Postcolonial Literatures and so on. Another example is the discipline of Engineering, which has a number of sub-disciplines, such as Mechanical Engineering, Electrical Engineering, Civil Engineering, Mining Engineering or Materials Engineering, which may have some subjects in common, such as Physics, but the majority of subjects are specific to the individual sub-discipline. In some disciplines, students enjoy the freedom of choosing which subjects they will study within the faculty offerings, but these typically must fit within a structured framework that requires a certain number of subjects to be taken in the final year (usually called '300 level' or '400 level'), and no more than a certain number of subjects at the introductory level (usually called '100 level') are to count towards the degree. In other disciplines the course of study is prescribed, as is typically the case in professional degrees (Medicine, Nursing, Education, Law and so on) and students have little room to veer from the prescribed path of study. Learning to operate successfully within each discipline involves the student taking on the *accoutrements* or trappings of the discipline; becoming part of the discipline 'culture'. More than simply learning a body of knowledge, students learn to understand the language of the discipline, to be able to read and write it with mastery, and, eventually, they are able fully to participate within the 'life' of the discipline. In this aspect, acquiring a university degree is a much deeper and more fulfilling process than simply undertaking 'training'; at the completion of the study, the graduate is changed inexorably.

## Discipline matches and mismatches

A 'match' between the discipline and the student occurs when the student has the intellectual capacity to acquire the knowledge and skills that are embodied within the discipline, and demonstrates no significant 'social or occupational' clinical impairment (American Psychiatric Association, 2013, p. 51) that prevents the student from full participation in the discipline culture. A good match also involves the student having a comfortable intellectual 'fit' with the body of knowledge: being mathematically inclined is helpful if the student is undertaking Engineering, Accountancy or Physics, and meeting the entry standards of having passed high-level high-school mathematics will always ensure the student has an easier path to success in the subject area and the discipline. A match with Arts entails the student having a love of, or facility with, reading and writing, since assessment tasks in Arts always involve the reading of a large body of works and the writing of sustained academic argument in the form of essays and dissertations. If a student is studying English Literature, then fluency in English itself is necessary, as is the capacity to interpret image, metaphor and all the other nuances of published writers. If a student is studying History, then a good match with the subject area will entail the student having the capacity to undertake detailed research involving reading historical documents and the works of historians and being able to draw inferences from disparate texts and a wide range of evidence. Most of the sub-disciplines in Humanities or Arts disciplines require students to have developed a set of highly functional social skills because they are required to discuss in tutorial groups the texts and research that they have read. The level of discussion involves articulating a case and presenting evidence for a particular position, accepting critical and opposing argument from others (without becoming upset that a contrary position has been put) and supporting and contributing to the arguments put by others. A good match with the professional disciplines such as Education, Medicine and Nursing would include having empathy, the ability to be socially appropriate, and to enjoy working with people; socially awkward people would have a struggle in most aspects of these disciplines because they need to have an absence of 'deficits in social communication and social interaction across multiple contexts' (American Psychiatric Association, 2013, p. 50). In these disciplines, '[i]nsistence on sameness, inflexible adherence to routines, or rituali[s]ed patterns of verbal or nonverbal behaviour' (American Psychiatric Association, 2013, p. 51) would render success in the practical aspect of the degrees unlikely.

A 'mismatch' can occur when a student has a 'clinically significant impairment in social, occupational, or other important areas of current functioning' (American Psychiatric Association, 2013, p. 51), as described above, such that it negatively impacts successful participation within the discipline. Mismatches can also occur between: what is offered at university or college as a degree course; what a student wishes to study; what a student thinks the degree course is all about; and whether the course aligns with the student's relative strengths or weaknesses. The mismatches can place the student's progress in the course in jeopardy and, as we will see in Chapter 3, sometimes they can lead to breaches of codes of conduct. Some students will enrol in an inappropriate degree course in the misguided belief that it relates exactly to their field of interest, when it bears no relationship to it – or only a tangential relationship to it, at best. Others will enrol in undergraduate degree programmes for which they have no interest or aptitude on the mistaken advice of family, friends, or university staff, or even on their own whim, believing it will lead to a particular qualification. Still others will enrol in subjects that require established prior knowledge (which, in our experience, is always published in advance of enrolment) and then engage in 'blaming' the institution, faculty or tutor when the subject or course fails to meet their expectations. These are common problems for students with Autism Spectrum Disorder and can occur in both undergraduate and postgraduate students because prior learning, such as in an undergraduate experience, is not necessarily transferred to a new situation, such as postgraduate learning.

## Mismatches between real and perceived requirements of degrees

There is often a world of difference between what a student perceives a degree will entail and what it actually entails. This may be attributed to youth or naiveté, but it is also symptomatic of students with Autism Spectrum Disorder. Universities, being mindful of the disability legislation, do not wish to be seen to discourage students from enrolling in their degrees of choice. However, no matter how understandable this position is, it fails to consider issues around rigidity of thinking, which means that some students are permitted to enrol in degree programmes for which it is seemingly apparent to everyone *but* the student that they are not suited. Unfortunately, in many countries, this leads to the student accruing a significant debt for tuition, which is predicated on the belief that the student will eventually be gainfully and professionally employed and able to repay the debt. Universities need to have sufficient mechanisms in place to well manage their duty of care in this regard by better advising students throughout their courses if there are progress challenges up to and including an unlikelihood of eventual success and graduation.

### Eva

*Within two minutes of beginning our first appointment, Eva shouted at me that she had Asperger's Syndrome and a 'MENSA-level IQ'. She had enrolled at university following a protracted enrolment in an Art course at a local vocational college. She had never completed high school. At university she had been granted enrolment in a degree in Physics on the basis of her certificate qualification, even though Art and Physics are disciplines with little in common. Physics requires pre-requisite Mathematics knowledge and a pass in final-year high school mathematics (or equivalent) at an advanced level, which was not something Eva possessed. In the first year she failed MATH101 and was allowed to repeat. Following her second attempt, she failed again and was excluded from the university. The Course Co-ordinator advised her to return to the vocational college to complete pre-requisite mathematics, which she did, and then she returned (triumphantly) to re-enrol. She again failed MATH101 and was offered one-to-one support from the Course Co-ordinator and the Learning Development Mathematics Lecturer, with whose intensive, individualised support she managed to pass the subject and to enrol in MATH102, the second subject in the Maths strand of the course. Predictably, she failed again.*

In this instance, Eva's assertiveness around having a 'MENSA-level IQ' was interpreted as an indication that she was sensitive to being potentially misunderstood as 'stupid', simply because she had been referred to Learning Development. She did not want the Learning Development lecturer to think that she was anything other than highly intelligent, a concept that is recognised in the literature (Attwood, 2007; Carrington and Graham, 2001; Carrington, Papinczak and Templeton, 2003). Eva's determination to undertake the course in Physics, while admirable, was actually working against her. Her rigid thinking caused her to persist with a degree programme for which she demonstrated little aptitude. All the evidence suggested that her academic strengths did not lie in Mathematics and Sciences. Indeed, she had taken a few Arts subjects and had received Distinction and High Distinction grades, but the Humanities were not what she wished to study.

### Eva

*Eva revealed that she had developed a theory that would radically change the way the world viewed the natural order. She claimed it would be as ground-breaking as Einstein's Theory of Relativity; however, she felt that she had to complete a Physics degree in order to have credibility when later she sought to publish this theory. In order to share her ideas with physicists, she reasoned, she first had to have the language of Physics.*

The idea that Eva had a MENSA-level IQ was not inconceivable for those of us who had read her writing, but was less believable for her Mathematics teachers. It is also important to note that while students on the spectrum are often encouraged into Science, Technology, Engineering and Maths (STEM) because this is stereotypically the comfort zone for those on the spectrum, some individuals with Autism Spectrum Disorder may have strengths in the literary and fine arts (Norris, 2014).

Some students may also have relative strengths in some areas of STEM, but not others.

### Rachel

*Rachel was in her final three subjects of a Civil Engineering degree when she was referred to Learning Development. She did not act on the referral at the time, but made an appointment several weeks later, by which time it was apparent (at least to her teachers) that she was on track to fail all three subjects.*

*At our first appointment, Rachel appeared dressed in pink from head to toe, and wearing a baseball cap with a logo on it that referred to a popular children's toy from Mattel. It was as though she had found a style with which she was comfortable as a child, and had continued with it into her mid-twenties, even though it was socially somewhat inappropriate for the semi-professional context of the university, and would certainly be inappropriate if she wore it on her final placement.*

> *Rachel reported that she had been very good at Mathematics at school, leading to her enrolment in the Engineering course. She reported that she still did well with 'Maths and formulas [sic] and things', but that she had problems in exams when she was asked to do 'triangle thingy-s'.*

It would seem that Rachel had strengths in areas of Mathematics, but not within Applied Trigonometry, which is generally considered to be a crucial element of Engineering studies. It was hard to imagine that Rachel would soon be eligible to work as a professional civil engineer; it also seemed as though timely course counselling might have seen her enrol in a more theoretical maths or science course, rather than one in which a miscalculation could cause a very serious public safety issue.

## Multiple intelligences and their role in matches and mismatches

Gardner's concept of 'Multiple Intelligences' is helpful in providing an explanation for the co-existence of Autism Spectrum Disorder and high intelligence or even giftedness (Gardner, 1993, 1999; Norris, 2014). Gardner identifies eight distinct intelligences: visual-spatial; bodily-kinaesthetic; musical; interpersonal; intrapersonal; linguistic; logical-mathematical (these seven outlined in *Frames of Mind* in 1983); and naturalist intelligence (added in *Intelligence Reframed: Multiple Intelligences for the Twenty-First Century* in 1999). According to Gardner's theory, we understand the world and ourselves by using all of these intelligences, but we differ from each other in the relative strengths of each type of intelligence, and in how we utilise them to learn, to solve problems and to engage with the world.

Visual-spatial intelligence describes the ability to understand physical space, such as in Architecture and Engineering, and lends itself to teaching and learning through the use of drawings and verbal and physical imagery, including graphics, charts, photographs and a range of multimedia. Bodily-kinaesthetic intelligence involves effective use of the body and body awareness, as do students of Sport Science, Drama and Dance, and well utilises movement, touching, equipment and objects as teaching/learning tools. Those favouring musical intelligence display sensitivity to rhythm and sound. They may enjoy learning with music playing in the background or make use of rhythmic ways of learning, such as through song lyrics or tapping out tempos. Interpersonal intelligence involves understanding and interacting with others. Since it involves having a highly developed sense of empathy, it is well utilised in group-learning situations, such as seminars and tutorials, and online conferencing. Intrapersonal intelligence is displayed by independent learners and involves understanding one's own interests and goals. It is expressed in having wisdom, intuition, motivation, confidence and the ability to express opinions. Linguistic intelligence is self-explanatory; having the ability to use words effectively. It is displayed in people with highly developed auditory skills and those who have facility with reading, writing, computers, foreign languages and word games. Those with high linguistic intelligence can be found in all of the sub-disciplines of Humanities. Logical-mathematical intelligence, like linguistic intelligence, is self-explanatory. People with this strength have facility with thinking conceptually and abstractly and identifying patterns and relationships in and between data. They enjoy reasoning and calculating, experimenting, solving puzzles and playing logic games, and can be found in abundance in disciplines such as Mathematics, Statistics, Science, Computing Science, Engineering and Architecture. The final intelligence, naturalist intelligence, relates to the ability to perceive patterns in nature, to understand how we relate to the environment, and to identify how to use it.

Gardner's theory of multiple intelligences is an advance on earlier definitions of intelligence and utilises a wider base of evidence. It provides a useful framework for conceptualising how, within universities, we can utilise the relative strengths presented by our students with Autism Spectrum Disorder. As we can see in the case study of Eva, and others that follow in this book, there are uneven cognitive profiles among individuals on the spectrum (Attwood, 1998; Barnhill, Hagiwara, Myles and Simpson, 2000; Cash, 1999; Foley-Nipcon, Assouline and Stinson, 2012; Minshew, Goldstein and Siegel, 1997; Norris, 2014; Sciutto, Richwine, Mentrikoski and Niedzwiecki, 2012). In your teaching, it is unlikely that you will come across students on the spectrum with highly developed interpersonal intelligence or intrapersonal intelligence, since these are the areas where people on the spectrum typically have difficulty. Strengths, or even giftedness, are distinctly possible within any of the other intelligences.

## Mismatches between previous and current study

There was a mismatch between what postgraduate student Jacqueline had as *a priori* qualifications, knowledge and experience and the degree in which she – perhaps mistakenly – had been granted enrolment.

### Jacqueline

*Jacqueline, who had Bachelor degrees in Economics and Computer Technology, was a fifty-something student with Autism Spectrum Disorder enrolled in a postgraduate coursework degree programme related to electronic music. She enjoyed electronically produced music and viewed it as just another aspect of computer technology. Undergraduate degrees in music clearly publicised that they required Level 8 music proficiency in any instrument prior to enrolment. Jacqueline did not know this as she had not read the undergraduate course requirements because she was enrolling in a postgraduate course. She had no background in music and did not play an instrument, but on the basis of her previous degree successes was granted admission to this postgraduate degree. She spent two traumatic years blaming her teachers for not 'starting at the beginning (by teaching her music)' and sought to teach herself music in order to keep up with subjects that required her to compose music, electronically. She became very anxious and depressed but could not be persuaded to withdraw from the programme. Despite long periods of absence on medical grounds, she continued with the degree. Eventually, the Course Co-ordinator (fearful of adverse publicity and viewing the situation as a 'one off') provided alternative assessment tasks and huge amounts of teaching support that allowed her to complete the course with sufficient credits to graduate. Enrolment procedures were later altered to include the provision of evidence of proficiency in music for postgraduate coursework degree programmes that required it.*

Jacqueline had high level 'linguistic intelligence', was a very experienced writer of academic text and, like Eva, wrote exceptionally high quality essays that allowed her markers to see what an intelligent and capable student she was. However, the level of anxiety she periodically experienced left her debilitated and unable to engage with the degree course in which she was enrolled. Attwood describes anxiety of the type experienced by Jacqueline as fluctuating in '"waves" with periods of intense panic, followed by a period of relative calm… The person may cope with their anxiety by retreating into their special interest' (Attwood, 1998, p. 154). Indeed, Bradshaw argues that anxiety is such a significant part of the profile of students on the spectrum that it must be borne in mind at all times when working with this cohort (Bradshaw, 2013). There were times when Jacqueline could make some headway, usually following extra tutorials provided by various tutors and lecturers in her course, who endeavoured to provide what was needed to scaffold her learning and to supplement her level of knowledge in music.

Sadly, this kind of situation is not unusual. Another case in point was James, who was in receipt of a disability pension because of his Autism Spectrum Disorder. James qualified for enrolment at university through a non-traditional pathway; on the basis of successful completion of a Technical and Further Education (TAFE) level Certificate course that was unrelated to any of the degrees offered at the university. In other words, he was given entry; but to what?

### James

*Despite excellent grades at high school in some subjects, notably English, James's overall final grade was insufficient for entry to university and he undertook a part-time practical Certificate-level course at a local TAFE that involved graphic design and a range of subjects applicable to working in a design workshop. Despite not eventuating in a diploma qualification, his level of pass was sufficient to lead to consideration and placement in the university at age 25. Like Jacqueline, his interest was electronic music production, but in James's case it was in audio mixing (he had created a CD of track mixes – unattributed to the originators of the tracks) or being a disc jockey ('DJ'). Again, like Jacqueline, he did not play an instrument and had little knowledge of music. With no university-level course leading to being a DJ available to him, he was advised to enrol in a Creative Arts degree with a major in Graphic Design, since he had done a little of this in his Certificate course.*

*On James's first day in the Graphic Design course, all students were assigned to computers in a laboratory and given an introductory project on which to work. James arrived late to class, looked around at all the other students working independently on their computers and felt overwhelmed. He screamed and ran from the room.*

James had done the 'right' things in terms of transition; at the time of enrolment he had disclosed his disability and registered with Disability Services. Even after the emotionally charged incident that saw him run from the classroom, he calmed down enough to consider his next move and, quite reasonably, went to consult with his Disability Liaison Officer.

### James

*Given James's response to his very first class, his Disability Liaison Officer advised him to explore his course options with his academic advisor. The outcome was enrolment in a Visual Arts degree offered by the same faculty. This, too, proved problematic, with James having no background in visual arts and the classroom codes and conventions being beyond his ken. One of his lecturers was interested in experimental classroom practices, which included workshops with tactile experiences, such as students rolling in paint, or, indeed, throwing it at each other. Unsurprisingly, James found these overly sensory practices to be over-stimulating and confronting. Even in the more conventional aspects of his studies, some of the artistic and theoretical concepts were so abstract as to be completely opaque to him. It was at this point that he was referred by his Disability Liaison Officer to seek assistance from the university's Learning Development unit.*

Learning Development support often involved working with James to 'decode' the requirements of his written assessment tasks that frequently involved esoteric or, to James, arcane concepts. We would work through, in great detail, a list of 10 or 12 essay topics, discussing in plain language what each question was asking and, therefore, what it would require him to research. Eventually, we would arrive at a consensus decision about which question was best for him to address; however, this decision was sometimes based on which question was most simple or pragmatic to answer, rather than those questions that would 'stretch' his thinking and allow him to demonstrate his high 'linguistic intelligence' (Gardner, 1993) and advanced capacity as a writer.

### *James*

*One assignment sought to have students identify and discuss 'creative spaces' and to suggest why they were useful as sites of creative endeavour. Examples were provided to the class, with one such example being the local shopping mall. James visited the shopping mall and reported that he had had a 'meltdown' trying to deal with the size of the place and being unable to determine which wall or building or area he could imagine would be useful as a creative space – no doubt because each surface was already in use, so literally were ruled out as potentially imaginatively available. He fled again, unsure of what to do to meet the requirements of the assignment.*

*Following a long session with me, where the idea of creative spaces was discussed in a broad context, James identified and settled on the idea of non-physical spaces. Over the next week he wrote an essay on 'the body as a creative space', discussing the contemporary fascination with tattoos and included a discussion of the metaphoric 'creative space between his ears'. The essay was awarded a High Distinction.*

James disclosed that he had experienced severe depression in the past, for which he had been hospitalised. Attwood addresses this, outlining the classic signs as 'clear changes in mood, appetite, sleep, and suicidal thoughts and actions… The person can become very introspective and critical of themselves in relation to the day's events' (Attwood, 1998, p. 159), and notes that clinical depression as a response to difficulties with social integration can occur as early as childhood in individuals on the spectrum (Attwood, 2007). It became obvious to us, the longer we knew him, that James's enrolment mismatch, that is, undertaking a Visual Arts major when he was not a practising visual artist and had low level 'visual-spatial intelligence' (Gardner, 1993), was creating high anxiety and depression. This all came to a head one day when James disclosed an obviously suicidal thought. This suicidal ideation was immediately reported to his nominated Counsellor, and a plan was enacted to convince him of a better 'match' with a different degree: English Literature in the Arts Faculty. This took a lot of explaining, and James took a lot of convincing: he had already had two starts – Graphic Design and Visual Arts – and he was hesitant to leave behind the few students with whom he had developed trust, despite the mismatch with his expectations of the subject. Besides, he was doing OK: he had got a High Distinction for his last essay! James finally agreed to the move when it was pointed out that English Literature would require lots of reading (which he enjoyed) and discussing other people's writing, but ultimately the subject area required students to 'read this' and 'write about that' (an area in which he had some demonstrated talent). Nevertheless, there were still some concerns: James had high 'linguistic intelligence', which would stand him in good stead in the discipline, but more problematic was his low level 'interpersonal intelligence', which would mitigate against success when he was required to discuss literature in groups in tutorial situations. Although not a straightforward decision, James agreed to change disciplines to a better match – no more malls, no more rolling in paint, and, it was hoped, no more anxiety and suicidal ideation. He still referred to the CD he had constructed and to the one brief DJ 'gig' he had secured for himself, but he accepted that the university could not formally offer him anything in that regard.

## Mismatches between Autism Spectrum Disorder traits and professional courses

Students can experience a mismatch between the course in which they choose to enrol and what better suits their skills, abilities and intelligences.

### Esther

*Esther was awarded a full scholarship to undertake her Bachelor's degree on the basis of extremely high achievement in the final examinations at high school. Her high school was well aware of her Autism Spectrum Disorder and had provided significant support throughout her six years with them, mainly for social difficulties, not academic issues. She enrolled in an Arts degree, majoring in History, a subject area with which she had a good match. She had a high level capacity for researching detailed items of historical evidence and well-developed academic writing ability. Despite these capacities, she obsessed over her assessment tasks and would stay awake for days as she worked on them, a behaviour that was both unusual in intensity and ultimately unnecessary. Her three years of her Bachelor's degree were marked by the high grades she achieved (she was placed on the Dean's Merit List, as was expected) and the considerable frustration and aggravation she evoked in those who interacted with her on a daily basis. She was incapable of not losing her purse, her door keys, her research materials, her mobile phone, nor of not missing the bus home – and solutions to all of this involved staff in Learning Development, Disability Services and Counselling. Esther was ideally suited to research in the Humanities and to undertaking an Honours degree and eventually a PhD. However, Esther was part of a Christian outreach group that sought to assist new arrival migrants by providing classes in English language, so following the awarding of her Bachelor degree, she instead chose to enrol in a Graduate Diploma TESOL in order to teach English as a Second Language to adult new arrival migrants. This was an obvious mismatch.*

Contemporary teaching methods utilise 'student-centred learning', which requires that the teacher have empathy and be able to 'read' the room; to be flexible and aware of the needs of learners, and to be able to anticipate and respond to their learning needs in a timely way. In practice, good teachers have highly developed 'interpersonal intelligence' (Gardner, 1993) and therefore are able to read the faces and body language of their students and to anticipate what they are thinking and the areas with which they are struggling. This is something with which people on the spectrum typically have significant difficulty. Attwood describes this as difficulty in acknowledging, praising, interesting or seeking clarification, reading body language or signifying the end of an utterance (Attwood, 1998; Baron-Cohen, 1995; Tantam, 2003). Tantam, Holmes and Cordess cite the difficulty people with Autism Spectrum Disorder have in making eye contact when another person is talking, and some who are on the spectrum have identified the difficulty they experience in listening to others, or in maintaining eye contact, stating that it breaks their concentration when they are attempting to listen to others (Tantam, Holmes and Cordess, 1993). Unfortunately, as Attwood points out, when an adult has difficulty making eye contact, this is often viewed with suspicion by neurotypical members of the public (Attwood, 2007). Making and maintaining eye contact and having the ability to listen to others are primary capacities for teachers, and it was clear to us that Esther undertaking a Graduate Diploma in Teaching English as a Second or Other Language (TESOL) in order to teach English language to adult migrants was a clear mismatch, since these were areas with which she had great difficulty.

### Esther

*Esther enjoyed the linguistic and other theoretical aspects of the Grad. Dip. TESOL and received high grades. She also enjoyed the preparation for her periods of practice teaching and took care to address all the academic requirements of teachers. What proved very difficult for her was: preparing lessons for adults, who would question and challenge the purpose of the exercises set; being flexible enough to change direction when the class required it – she would stick rigidly to her prepared lessons despite all indications that she should veer from her prepared script; making eye contact and knowing when her students were struggling; moving around the room in a comfortable manner in order to engage with her students to oversee the language exercises they were doing; accepting that learners work at different paces and there is a need for some students to return to ideas already covered; understanding that teaching a language involves the capacity to transfer cultural understandings as well as linguistic ones; being professionally tidy with the materials she prepared and handed out to students (untidy, scrunched up, unclean papers are unacceptable); and understanding the professional level of dress required of a teacher.*

Esther passed her course, since she did very well in the theoretical aspects and the practical aspects each involved 'pass/fail' criteria, which she clearly demonstrated she had met. What more 'seasoned' teachers critiqued, instead, was the likelihood of her being able to develop into an *effective* teacher, but this was not something that was assessed under the marking rubric. Beginning teachers are provided with the 'benefit of the doubt'; that is, it is accepted by their mentors that pre-service teachers are just beginning, or at the point of starting out as a teacher, and that they will develop classroom abilities, skills and capacities over time. For those with Autism Spectrum Disorder, however, it is highly unlikely that the required abilities and skills will develop at the expected rate (if at all) and, typically, teaching becomes too difficult. Effective teaching is dependent upon teachers having highly developed interpersonal and intrapersonal intelligences, to use Gardner's terminology.

Some universities have established a mechanism where a Dean or other senior member of faculty can dis-enrol a student who has demonstrated incapacity to complete a practical component of a professional degree programme (such as Teaching, Nursing or Medicine). This could be extended to other non-practicum based degree programmes. However, sometimes discipline mismatches can sort themselves out as time goes on and the difficulty becomes ineluctable to the person involved. Two case studies come to mind here.

### Peter

*Peter was in the final year of the professional Bachelor of Teaching (Science) degree in order to teach Science to high school students when he was referred to Learning Development by his Disability Liaison Officer. Peter was struggling with theoretical subjects in Education that addressed classroom dynamics, as well as the more esoteric aspects of Educational Psychology and Educational Practice. He was doing well in Physics and Chemistry. It was clear to us that he was a very literal thinker and that his obvious social difficulties would prove a problem in a classroom of 30 high school students. When asked, gently, why he wanted to teach, he reported that he had experienced great difficulty at high school, but that a Science teacher had helped him and was kind to him. He wanted to 'help other kids, like his teacher had' helped him. Written assessments of his classroom micro-teaching showed Peter was struggling at all levels and was in danger of failing. When it was suggested to him that he was very good at Physics and Chemistry and would be best to change to a Science degree, he became hostile. He managed to scrape through the degree and a year later, following several dreadful experiences of casual teaching and unlikely to ever be confirmed as a 'fully fledged' teacher, he returned to the university to complete a Science degree. He said, 'I realise now that I can't teach.'*

Medicine is another area that requires students to demonstrate a certain level of interpersonal intelligence and appropriate social skills, even if they have every intention of entering a specialisation that does not require those skills.

### Yari

*Yari, who had Autism Spectrum Disorder, had successfully completed a Bachelor of Bio-Medical Science (Honours) degree wherein he demonstrated high-level Logical-Mathematical intelligence. He wished to enrol in the combined degrees, Bachelor of Medicine/Bachelor of Surgery that were only available to graduates. Enrolment required successful completion of an 'objective' test that focused, among other things, on the candidate's ability and fluency in the English language (Linguistic intelligence) and logical capacity (Logical-Mathematical intelligence). As well as this, candidates were required to undertake an interview with a panel of Medical academics (interpersonal intelligence). In order to prepare for the interview, Yari rehearsed with an academic member of staff that he knew well, and who was familiar with the kinds of questions he would be asked. Despite the academic realising that Yari was unsuited to the interpersonal aspects of Medicine because of his lack of Theory of Mind, social awkwardness and inability to respond spontaneously to others' behaviours or in unfamiliar situations, he was rehearsed sufficiently well enough to compensate for these shortcomings – or to mask them. He was successful with both the test and the interview – and was offered a place in Medicine. Over the next five years he completed the double degree. When it came time to undertake his hospital residency years, because of his failure to adequately display empathy in a socially acceptable way – relevant to the context – he had significant difficulty relating to patients and hospital staff, being unable to make eye contact and unable to fully understand information if it was in auditory mode. This made the diagnostic process difficult for Yari, particularly because he was unable to establish trust with the patient or to elicit the level of information that he needed to support diagnosis.*

It is clear that some professions, such as Teaching, Nursing and Medicine, require high-level skills in 'reading' not only people's words, but also body language and emotion. What is required – and what may be lacking in those on the spectrum – is the ability to 'attribute mental states – beliefs, emotions, thoughts and bodily sensations – to oneself, and other people' (Norris, 2014, p. 39). Commonly termed 'empathy', researchers title this ability 'Theory of Mind' (Baron-Cohen, 1995; Baron-Cohen and Wheelwright, 2004; Frith, 2001; Norris, 2014; Perner, Frith, Leslie and Leekam, 1989), and it is 'closely associated with the educational literature on metacognition, which is the ability to mentally represent one's *own* thoughts and feelings' (Sodian and Frith, 2008, p. 39). Depending on where on the spectrum an individual sits, having a difficulty with Theory of Mind could mean that entry to some professions will ultimately be an unattainable goal. Although the development of compensatory mechanisms, such as memorising lists of '"rules" for social interactions to compensate for lack of intrinsic Theory of Mind' (Norris, 2014, p. 41) can be useful in some instances, they can not take the place of having a typically developed Theory of Mind, as in neurotypical individuals (Bowler, 1992; Williams, 2004). Professions such as Teaching, Nursing and Medicine require a highly developed Theory of Mind in order for the professional to understand the needs and expectations of the client group, and are often outside the practicality of students with Autism Spectrum Disorder, since '[l]ack of T[heory] o[f] M[ind] will be socially restrictive in tasks requiring spontaneous, advanced T[heory] o[f] M[ind]' (Norris, 2014, p. 42).

Sometimes when given time, social maturity, supportive relationships, and involvement with 'more capable others' (Gallimore and Tharp, 1990, p. 184), the professional with Autism

Spectrum Disorder can acquire stronger capacities in the area of interpersonal and intrapersonal intelligence.

### Yari

*Over time, Yari developed noticeable empathy for patients' wellbeing and for their care, as he demonstrated in the attention he paid to empathetic supportive protocols for patients in their end-of-life stages.*

Vygotsky's theory of cognitive development relied on the key concept of 'internalisation' (Langford, 2005, p. 35). He argued that all higher psychological processes are originally social processes, shared between people, such as children and adults or between instructors and learners. The novice first experiences active problem-solving activities in the presence of others but gradually comes to perform these functions independently. The 'distance' between what a learner is capable of doing unaided, and what the learner is capable of doing with the assistance, guidance or collaboration of more capable peers, is what Vygotsky titled the 'Zone of Proximal Development' (Vygotsky, Cole, John-Steiner, Scribner and Souberman, 1978, pp. 85–86). The Zone of Proximal Development can be thought of, in geographic terms, as learning 'terrain' to be crossed by the learner in order to reach some knowledge position predetermined by others; a position of mastery that may include the attainment of certain skills or the acquisition of certain knowledge (Gluck and Draisma, 1997, pp. 11–13). The process of internalisation is gradual; first the instructor or knowledgeable peer controls and guides the learner's activity, but gradually the instructor and the learner come to share the problem-solving and guiding. Finally, the instructor cedes control to the learner and functions primarily as a supportive and sympathetic audience (Gallimore and Tharp, 1990; Gluck and Draisma, 1997; Wertsch, 1978). Internalisation occurs gradually over four stages:

Stage I: where performance is assisted by more capable others;

Stage II: where performance is assisted by the self...[but where] performance is [not] fully developed [n]or automati[s]ed;

Stage III: where performance is developed, automati[s]ed, and fossili[s]ed; and

Stage IV: where deautomati[s]ation of performance leads to recursion through the [stages].

(GALLIMORE AND THARP, 1990, PP. 184–186)

Being a practising doctor within the hospital system exposed Yari to a range of 'more capable others'. At the same time, he experienced 'conditions of learning' that facilitated his development and engagement as a learner (Cambourne and Turbill, 1987, p. 7). He was 'immersed' in the culture of the hospital at both the macro and micro levels. 'Demonstrations' of appropriate practices surrounded him. He responded to the 'expectations' of his colleagues that he would succeed as a doctor and he took 'responsibility' for his own learning. He refined his practice over time, a process Brian Cambourne and Jan Turbill describe as 'approximation' (Cambourne and Turbill, 1987, p. 7). He developed his competence through continued 'practice' as a doctor and through 'engagement' with the *milieu* of health care and health practitioners; in particular, he participated in mutual exchanges with experts in the field, which provided a feedback 'response' to his ongoing learning approximation (Cambourne and Turbill, 1987, p. 7).

While it is possible for students on the spectrum to develop both coping skills and professional skills over time, many students who enrol at university are young and still developing their 'workarounds' for social and academic situations. Most students are likely to be wedded to the idea of studying for the profession they have chosen and students on the spectrum are not known for their willingness to change, so any conversations about suitability or otherwise should be undertaken with the greatest of sensitivity. We would recommend that any such conversations do not occur between student and lecturer/tutor without prior consultation with and the physical presence of specialist staff. It is not a case of telling students, for example, that they cannot teach because they are on the spectrum – this would be both untrue and unlawful. Rather, it is true that in some instances (such as Esther's), a great deal of time and effort went into developing even rudimentary teaching skills, a point beyond which she was unlikely to progress because her disability and low level interpersonal intelligence prevented her displaying the higher order empathy or developing the mastery of teaching that is expected in the profession. In other cases, such as that of Peter, the particular individual will ultimately become aware that a discipline mismatch has occurred. Accepting that a longed-for career is not suitable is traumatic for anyone, but arguably particularly difficult for someone on the spectrum who is not used to being flexible in their thinking. Obviously, the sooner these issues are dealt with, the better the outcome (as in James's case, where he was able to transfer the credits he earned while in the Creative Arts courses to his new degree and was able to graduate with a recognised qualification, even if it were not the one he originally sought).

## Conclusion

Finding a suitable match with a university discipline is not always easy and does not always follow, as a matter of course, from appropriate decisions made during high school. Family and social pressures or portrayals of particular disciplines or professions in the media can influence students to undertake a particular course of study or enrol in a certain degree. For those with Autism Spectrum Disorder, making initial discipline choices – and perhaps later making changes to those discipline choices – can be a difficult process, since it involves a deep understanding of one's own interests and goals, an understanding of what each discipline entails, including what 'goes on' at the classroom level, and a realistic grasp of one's own capacities. This requires a broad understanding of the professions and fields of knowledge, something that is not necessarily part of each student's family or social background, and certainly not something that can be fully grasped by watching television (we do understand, however, that television portrayals of hospital and legal dramas are influential in the high number of students seeking to enter the faculties of Medicine and Law). Students with Autism Spectrum Disorder can more easily than their neurotypical classmates make inappropriate discipline choices and, having made those choices, are more inclined to stick rigidly to them, often at their own peril in terms of eventually achieving academic success. University academic staff, such as Learning Development lecturers, are well-placed to discuss with students on the spectrum the discipline choices they have made, and where appropriate, to assist them to make more suitable choices.

## Tips for Teachers

- Take the time to become familiar with Gardner's 'Multiple Intelligences' and try to incorporate teaching and learning activities that cater to students who may have different 'intelligences'. Become aware of your own preferred 'intelligence' and how this affects your teaching style.

- Universities have a 'duty of care' towards all students, including a duty of care not to have them accrue tuition debts for courses that they cannot, within reason, complete. If, because of a disability, a student is unable to undertake the practical aspects of professional courses, then some institutions have rules governing enrolment that permit a very senior member of academic staff to dis-enrol the student. If you suspect that you have a student who might be better suited to a different course, we advise you to consult with more senior members of staff who have the authority and experience to enact the appropriate processes.

- If you identify a student whom you suspect has a mismatch with the discipline, a discussion with the Head of Students for your faculty, or other senior staff member who has responsibility for the welfare of students, is advisable.

- When raising with the student the idea that perhaps a discipline mismatch has occurred, do so gently (but directly – avoid metaphors!).

- Where possible, enlist the advice of the Disability Liaison Officer and/or Counselling Staff, and keep in mind current anti-discrimination and disability legislation. Choose your words carefully!

- Even when a mismatch has occurred, we still have a legal and ethical responsibility to teach all the students enrolled in our courses.

- Collate possible helpful resources or information on support services and share them with your students – all of them. Those who are most in need are also the least likely to be able identify that they have a need, or to find the time, energy or wherewithal to locate them for themselves.

- If you have students who have identified as being on the Autism Spectrum, take the time to meet with them individually to discuss the assessment tasks for the subject. Discuss what each question is asking (and not asking) and make suggestions for appropriate areas of research. Consider the possibility of offering to read an early draft of the student's work in order to make suggestions.

## Tips for Learners

- Take the time to become familiar with Gardner's 'Multiple Intelligences' and try to identify your most favoured and least favoured learning styles.

- Identify how 'intelligences' affect your learning and your participation in classroom activities.

- Try to develop learning strategies that cater to your favoured learning style.

- Make an appointment with a Learning Development staff member to get help in developing learning strategies that favour your identified learning style.

- Develop 'workarounds' for the areas/intelligences that you find most difficult (again, a Learning Development Lecturer can help with this if it seems daunting).

- Understand that all university disciplines lend themselves to particular student learning styles and intelligences, and that the best 'match' with a discipline will occur when student qualities align with the discipline requirements.

- It is important that you assess your situation. If you feel that you are experiencing a mismatch with the discipline in which you are enrolled, talk to a Learning Development Lecturer, an Academic Advisor, a Disability Liaison Officer or a Student Counsellor. They will discuss with you the course choices you have made and can assist you to find resources to help or a more comfortable discipline match. Some students decide to discontinue in a particular discipline, while other students decide to continue, and to seek support from suitable professionals.

- Make regular appointments with a Learning Development Lecturer to discuss your assessment tasks and the progress you are making toward completing them. It is best to have your first appointment for each semester by the end of Week 2, where possible.

# Chapter 3

# Interpreting Expectations and Codes of Conduct

## Introduction

Having established some contexts about the tertiary environment, students on the spectrum, learning, and what happens when these things collide, let us now turn very explicitly to the university, classroom, and expectations about conduct. Educational institutions, at all levels, have written and unwritten codes of conduct for students. The written codes of conduct, typically, have been developed by staff committees and refer to behaviour, or more specifically, inappropriate behaviour, such as cheating or non-attendance. Typically, too, they focus on penalties for that inappropriate behaviour, such as exclusion from class or from the institution. The unwritten or implied codes of conduct, however, are cultural. They develop over time and relate to how the institution or a classroom functions: how lectures, tutorials, seminars, workshops, practical classes and other learning environments differ; how students and teachers participate; who speaks when; how to make a comment or engage in debate; how to ask a question; how to rebut an argument; how to speak with faculty staff; how to dress when attending. These implied codes of conduct may differ from one academic discipline to another and from one teacher to another, but they demonstrate a common thread: how to participate and how to be well mannered in the classroom so that all students are best positioned to learn. Learning what is appropriate, and what is not, is particularly difficult for students with Autism Spectrum Disorder when the codes of conduct are unwritten, implied or tacit.

## Assisting students to adapt their behaviour to university

We often think of students on the spectrum as 'academically bright but socially inept' (Bradshaw, 2013, p. 20), which can make navigating university extremely difficult, but it is important to remain mindful that 'having Asperger's Syndrome does not stop people from learning and developing their knowledge or skills' (Bradshaw, 2013, p. 47). As university teachers, it is incumbent upon us to assist students to learn to adapt to the university environment. University comes with a new set of expectations, new rules and even new classrooms and types of classes. It also comes with a new set of expectations about their teachers; what they do, how they do it, and what they expect of students, especially in terms of independent learning. Students often remark that it is not 'like anything they've done before' – those who have come from the Technical and Further Education (TAFE) system find the shift in pace and tone difficult, and for students matriculating from high school, it may feel like being dropped on another planet. For students on the spectrum who have learned the procedures and expectations in high school (and who may have had dedicated support aides – at least in Australia), the transition can be very difficult indeed. Routines and structure can be developed in high school through having a seating plan and regular teachers. At university, students must negotiate not only the different kinds of classes (lectures, tutorials, labs, seminars, workshops, practical classes), but also it is likely that at some point the student will find herself or himself in a large and noisy lecture theatre, unable to find a preferred seat in an exit row, and being addressed by a guest lecturer. This can trigger unwanted behaviours and anxiety in the student (and others!).

For some students, 'shifting gears' between subjects may be problematic; for others, the longer periods for which they are expected to concentrate (such as two-hour lectures) may prove to be too much for their attention spans. For all students beginning at university, there is some degree of culture shock and there is a significant amount of 'hidden curriculum'. The university or college environment is generally understood to be an adult independent learning environment and it is assumed that students will quickly come to understand the requirements of this learning environment because they will have developed the social skills to do so. It is further assumed that students will be independent learners with the desire and capacity to learn, have an ability to self-monitor and a capacity to socialise, often within the artificial constraints of classroom discussion and groupwork. Limitations in any of the above areas can lead to marginalisation. In high school, the main concern about deficits in social skills is that they can lead to bullying and exclusion (Davies, 2014). While the risk of bullying is diminished within the adult learning environment, there is an added complication in that classroom requirements are inextricably linked with learning and assessment; because of the prevalence of group learning tasks and group assessments, social skills (or lack of them) can impact on academic outcomes. Students on the spectrum will need to develop the required social skills if they are to succeed in their chosen fields of study, a requirement that depends on the student having well-developed interpersonal intelligence (Gardner, 1993, 1999). The variety of situations, both learning and social, requires a range of behaviours in order for the student to fit in and a range of spoken 'registers' (varying in levels of formality, for instance) in order to fully participate. If this aspect of transition does not go well and the student fails to pick up on the tacit cues of the discipline and classroom culture, then she or he may be branded as 'odd' or a 'troublemaker' for the duration of study.

The first issue for many students is one of nomenclature; it is extraordinary how many students, when asked during orientation activities, do not know the difference between a lecture and a tutorial. This has obvious implications since these two learning environments have quite different behavioural expectations. Lectures are where the lecturer lectures and students listen and take notes. Sometimes they are able to ask questions and may be invited to do so either at the end of the lecture or at identified points throughout, but mostly no interruption to the lecturer is welcome. Lectures vary in the size of audience and may range from a small group to hundreds of students. Many individuals on the spectrum have difficulty in delineating which information is salient and which is 'background...noise' (Wolf, Thierfeld Brown and Kukiela Bork, 2009, p. 229), and so may experience a large lecture hall more as a distracting cacophony than a place of learning.

Tutorials typically involve 20 or more students, who are in close proximity (often around a large table or nests of tables) and in close interaction with each other and the tutor. The tutor may also be the lecturer for the subject, or more often will be appointed only to tutor and assess, but needs to be aware of each student's capacity. Students need to be mindful of all other learners' expectations. They need to have well-developed interpersonal and linguistic intelligences (Gardner, 1993, 1999); be able to 'get into' the conversation; to know when to keep out of it; and, at all times, they need to be polite. Tutorials essentially require a well-developed understanding of group dynamics, something with which a number of people on the spectrum often express difficulty (Holliday Willey, 1999). Indeed, Attwood argues that people on the spectrum are 'primarily individuals, rather than natural team members' (Attwood, 2007, p. 121). Attwood further describes 'adults with Asperger's Syndrome who have asked people not to speak when they are considering what to say in reply to a question as this [would] disrupt their thought processes and further delay their reply' (Attwood, 1998, p. 85). Most tutors would have difficulty acceding to this request as it would completely disrupt the flow of the tutorial discussion. Many students will quickly learn from context that the kind of interaction that is required in a tutorial is not welcomed in a mono-directional lecture; but, as we discussed in the introduction, students on the spectrum are often slower to learn from social context, so there is significant room for error and often it may be necessary for their teachers to help them navigate this terrain.

The lecture/tutorial model, common in universities, is based on the idea that students will have done the more passive learning – required readings and listening to lectures – prior to attending the more active learning space of the tutorial classroom. Again, this is rarely explained explicitly during orientation, so that even neurotypical students may not be aware of these implied expectations. Some tutors are seen as 'harsh' because they tell students that if they arrive unprepared and unable to contribute, they can expect to be politely asked to leave; that participation implies more than presence. In reality, this has always been an expectation but few tutors articulate or enforce the expectation. More often, assessment for some subjects includes a 'participation' mark, which is derived, subjectively, by the tutor on the basis of whether the student has made a contribution to the class, based on prior reading and lecture attendance, and demonstrated this through appropriate participation in class discussion or groupwork.

Beyond lectures and tutorials there is a variety of other learning situations common in universities, including seminars, workshops, laboratories, individual sessions, group learning and online learning. Seminars usually involve between 15 and 50 students, so it is necessary to be able to participate in this larger forum without behavioural or social glitches. Workshops and laboratories usually include a practical component (such as working in groups, developing a consensus argument, writing a group report, building models, or carrying out experiments). In each of these situations, as well as when working in an individual situation with a fellow student, tutor, lecturer or Learning Development Lecturer, students need to be able to work closely (but not intimately) with a range of people, so a solid grasp of language 'register', a person's 'academic rank', manners and behaviours are critical.

Other situations, such as online learning and online communication with other students or staff members, require students to be able to respond within this 'intimate' communication space without becoming inappropriately familiar or social. This can be particularly difficult to negotiate for younger students who have come to understand the socially acceptable ways of interacting on social media platforms such as Facebook, Twitter, Snapchat or Instagram, many of which would be wildly inappropriate on a subject-based educational platform hosted by the institution in which they are studying. Similarly, when undertaking written or oral assessment tasks, students need to be able to respond within a range of written and spoken genres without becoming inappropriately or overly formal, or, worse, familiar or social. They must also 'understand the perspective of the instructor so they can meet the expectations of an assignment or know how to answer an essay question on an exam' (Palmer, 2006, p. 50). Within the examination room students must be respectful of others' needs and have the ability not to look around the room, since this has the potential of the student being misunderstood by invigilators.

## Codes of conduct: students

When interpersonal and intrapersonal intelligences (Gardner, 1993, 1999) are low, people can have difficulty in understanding and interacting with others, in understanding their own interests and goals, which means there is potential for reduced ability to 'read' a situation, which, in turn, can lead to odd or inappropriate classroom behaviour. Indeed, it may sometimes breach established codes of conduct.

### Kenneth

*Kenneth was a forty-something male who cared for his mother and, despite significant intellect, had only held menial jobs. He gained direct entry to university through an interview process. Because of his ongoing carer's duties and financial difficulties, he sometimes missed class in order to go to his own or his mother's medical appointments. He knew that if he missed a class, he needed to contact the tutor and make arrangements for work in lieu. On one occasion, however, he came to a one-hour class some 45 minutes late. Because he had not missed the class, he did not apologise to the tutor. Instead, he came into the library class, interrupted the guest speaker, and went to a website other than the one the rest of the class were using — and one which had an audible and distracting soundtrack of some kind. When the tutor sidled up to Kenneth and advised him quietly that if he opted not to participate in class, he would be marked absent, Kenneth became enraged. To his mind, he was present and therefore he could not be marked absent. He began shouting and swearing about the injustice, and when the tutor went out to the main desk of the library to seek support, asked why she was calling security (which she had not, in fact, thought to do, since there was no permanent security presence on that small campus — clearly, Kenneth had been in similar situations before).*

*After leaving the campus with much fuss and fanfare, Kenneth later returned to argue with senior management about why the tutor was being unreasonable. At one point he was heard to shout, 'I don't mean to threaten you, but I know karate.'*

Clearly, none of Kenneth's behaviour was socially acceptable within a learning and teaching context. His rage and threats towards the tutor ultimately led to his being suspended from class and taught one-to-one by a senior academic on another campus, via videoconferencing software. Students on the spectrum are frequently branded as 'odd' or, worse, troublemakers, in university classrooms. Sometimes, because of the kinds of outbursts described above, they are feared as potentially being violent — even when there is no known history of such behaviour. For a neurotypical lecturer or student, these kinds of conclusions seem reasonable when a student utters the phrase, 'I don't mean to threaten you, but…'; takes out the newspaper and reads it in a lecture hall; insists that they must sit in a particular seat; interrupts the lecturer; or lies down on the floor of a tutorial classroom. It is unlikely that an adult student with autism is actually trying to draw attention through these behaviours, yet this is how they may be interpreted as the behaviours seem to be on a par with a toddler's tantrum. The more likely explanation, in reality, is that the student is wanting to ensure that an outburst of feelings will not be misconstrued; is feeling the need to withdraw, but knows that the expectation is that students should be present; is trying to avoid problems with light or acoustics that arise elsewhere in the lecture theatre; or has a back problem that requires stretching. Helping them to understand the social context may help to minimise such behaviours, as the students will at least understand that they are considered to be aberrant.

### James

*James demonstrated little regard for the power relationship between lecturer and student, both in the faculty and in Learning Development. He also had scant regard for his fellow students. He was guilty of interrupting tutorial presentations by fellow students, or taking weekly tutorial discussions to inappropriate 'places' and subjects in order to monopolise a starring role. He would interrupt lectures and seminars with inane (to others) tangents and questions, and was unable to be redirected to have his questions or needs met at some other time. On more than one occasion he lay supine on the tutorial room floor, rather than sit in a chair around a group table. To his teachers and fellow students this appeared to be infantile attention-seeking behaviour rather than an obvious indication that he was on the Autism Spectrum and needed support and clear direction to more appropriately respond to the classroom code of behaviour.*

*James's visits to Learning Development demonstrated that even in a one-to-one teaching context, he struggled with the conventions of behaviour. Inappropriate sexual references and innuendo were hallmarks of his early consultations and he appeared to delight in the one-to-one teaching context as an opportunity to experiment with verbal innuendo with his older female academic lecturer. He appeared to really misunderstand the codes and conventions of being a university student, and, in particular, how to behave in an adult academic environment.*

James's misbehaviour is not atypical but encapsulates several of the behaviours that we have experienced over many years. Several students with Autism Spectrum Disorder have lain on the floor or stood when it was more appropriate to sit like every other student in the room. Interrupting lectures or classroom teaching, or inappropriately interrupting fellow students who are undertaking oral presentations or engaging in established discussion, are very common occurrences. In the case of lying on the floor, one response might be to ignore inappropriate behaviour in the (vain) hope that it will stop, but this can be interpreted as tacit approval or, in the case of students with Autism Spectrum Disorder, become a trigger for more eccentric behaviour. A more useful response might be to invite the student to sit with the group, thereby providing the student with positive acknowledgement and immediately move on with the lesson. If the behaviour were to be repeated, you could request the student sit with the group and at the end of the lesson, take him or her aside and make it quite clear that in your classroom this is not acceptable behaviour. In the case of sexual innuendo or other inappropriate references, it is important to stop the behaviour before it gathers any momentum. If it has occurred within a classroom, then an immediate statement to the effect that this is not acceptable behaviour is the best course of action. Generally speaking, when this kind of thing occurs, classmates' body language will indicate that a 'line has been crossed', but the student with Autism Spectrum Disorder is unlikely to recognise that body language and to respond. In some circumstances, particularly if the student is a 'serial offender', it is not unusual for classmates to directly confront the student, who may not understand why he or she is being 'attacked'. Solving the situation will be simplest if it involves a direct intervention by the teacher, who can then privately (where possible) discuss the behaviour and suggest alternative and appropriate ways to behave.

Attwood suggests that a minority of students will be deliberately maladaptive or even macabre in their behaviours, in order to test the reactions of others; that there 'can be great delight in causing a dramatic response and achieving the ability to control and manipulate people's emotions' (Attwood, 1998, p. 60). When James's sexual innuendo occurred in the one-to-one teaching context in Learning Development, the staff member reported it to the Head, who then transferred all further appointments with him to herself, reasoning that James would be less likely to continue this behaviour with a more senior member of staff, one who might remind him of his grandmother! The strategy worked, but when this is not an available option, a direct statement that indicates sexual innuendo is not appropriate behaviour and that it is not welcome, is an effective first step. If it persists, then enquiring of Disability Services and/or Learning Development whether the student is registered with them is a discreet way of potentially initiating a discussion with the Disability Liaison Officer, if one is required. Beyond this, there are usually official channels for complaint that can be activated.

It can be very difficult if you are a casually paid, sessional tutor, who is confronted with these types of situation, since there is a perception that it is the more independent tutors who are offered 'repeat' work. Nevertheless, sexual harassment is a workplace safety issue that requires you to provide a safe learning environment for all students, and the institution is also required to provide you with a safe working environment. Dealing with the issue, as and when it arises, is critical to resolving it.

Knowing how to participate in a university classroom or how the code of conduct for that classroom operates can be arcane or opaque to the student with Autism Spectrum Disorder. Attwood sees the use of language in a social context and the ability to engage in the 'art of conversation' as an area that has particular difficulties for the child on the spectrum (Attwood, 1998, p. 68).

He identified that children with Autism Spectrum Disorder have issues with: repairing a conversation; coping with uncertainty or mistakes; overcoming a tendency to make irrelevant comments; knowing when not to interrupt; staying on track or coming back to the topic; and, desiring not to appear stupid (Attwood, 1998). For the university student with Autism Spectrum Disorder, these are also the main issues that arise within the classroom. Prime among them are interrupting other students when they are talking and making irrelevant comments that are not linked to the topic of conversation. The ability to identify momentary pauses or the end of the topic, or to recognise eye contact from the tutor that indicates 'now it's your turn to speak', may pose difficulties for the student. Irrelevant comments can often be the result of word associations or 'fragments of the dialogue of previous conversations or quite bizarre utterances' (Attwood, 1998, p. 70). Attwood suggests ignoring such interruptions and maintaining focus 'on the central theme of the conversation' (Attwood, 2007, p. 209). We have found that this strategy comes naturally to most classroom teachers and is preferable to focusing on the interruption and asking the student what he or she means. To do so only prolongs the interruption, keeps discussion off track and runs the risk of making the student feel stupid.

Students may also have trouble processing that a range of language 'registers' may be required. For example, a conversational tone might be completely appropriate in a tutorial situation, and a student on the spectrum might then think that this is an acceptable benchmark for the subject, rather than an acceptable benchmark for that particular learning context within the subject. If the student incorporates this rather casual tone when writing assessment tasks, however, he or she is likely to be disappointed by the mark received. Conversely, students with Autism Spectrum Disorder sometimes adopt an overly formal way of speaking and writing and this, too, can appear odd in the classroom or be sufficiently inappropriate in the written mode that it affects the assessment mark received. Again, these are not issues that are necessarily isolated to students on the spectrum, so proactively making expectations clear is likely to help a number of students. Whereas most students will learn from context how to appropriately address teaching staff (for example, in Australia, most class tutors and lecturers will be addressed by their first names after the initial introduction), students on the spectrum may agonise over why it is necessary to address an official email request to the subject co-ordinator with 'Dear Professor X…' when the same person is addressed as 'Charles' when working as a classroom-based tutor in the same subject. Students need to be taught these kinds of conventions, and as a teacher, the best solution is to simply announce on the first occasion that you meet in the semester how you would like to be addressed, and if there are any exceptions for specific contexts. Providing good examples of academic writing that clearly demonstrate the written register required will assist all students, including those on the spectrum.

## Codes of conduct for teachers

Most university lecturers and tutors have come to their profession as a result of their passion and success within a particular field of study. It may therefore not occur to us that some students have quite a different – and more difficult – learning experience. It is important to remember to start with thinking about your own teacher behaviours and what you can do (Wagner, 2002). It is far easier to make adjustments to your own behaviour and classroom environment than to deal with the fallout when a student who has a social disability, and may be resistant to change, is expected to know how and when to adapt his or her behaviour.

It can be easy to use a student's diagnosed difference to explain why they are not learning well, but in any learning/teaching relationship there are two protagonists whose behaviour can come under review. As the teacher, ultimately you are in both the more powerful and the more responsible position, and you are more likely to understand the social codes of the institution than a student on the spectrum. While you may attempt to influence your students' behaviour, you have total control over your own, so it is usually easier to start with reflecting on your practice. Are your instructions clear and concise? Are they consistent with school or faculty processes, so as to limit future confusion or contradiction? Are the students clear on what the consequences will be for non-attendance, non-compliance, non-preparation or non-submission? Are the students given enough time to process instructions or new information (Wagner, 2002)? Ultimately, when dealing with students who are both resistant to and/or have a reduced capacity for change, teachers will likely find it easier and more productive to alter their own behaviour and establish frameworks that increase the students' likelihood of success.

Six areas of academic staff education have been identified that will develop inclusion in an educational environment. These are being aware of social, philosophical and legal issues; keeping abreast of educational service delivery trends; positive and productive attitudes; sound educational interventions; adequate preparation of personnel, and research. In the highly casualised university sector, it can of course be difficult to make sure that all teaching staff members receive such workplace education. This book covers all six areas, with delivery trends, attitudes and interventions covered in detail in this chapter.

The established qualities sought when recruiting peer mentors to assist students on the spectrum also gives some insight into how best teachers can work with these students. These include having a calm personality and being able to recover quickly from unusual reactions or answers; an ability to understand the material and being able to convey critical information about it; and being consistent and stable in expectations and behaviour (Wagner, 2002). It is important to remember that although the student may 'look normal' – and indeed, may be intellectually gifted – the disability is real and it is not about the student being lazy or not caring about performance.

## Delivery trends

As noted in the introduction, in recent years there has been a shift towards groupwork, group assignments and other more 'creative' assessment tasks. While this is to be admired in terms of pedagogy, this particular trend also means that students on the spectrum are likely to require more support if they are to successfully complete their assessment tasks and, by extension, their degrees.

Groupwork requires students to communicate effectively with classmates, demonstrate sound organisational skills in order not to let down said teammates, and understand group dynamics – all areas within which many on the spectrum find some difficulty (Attwood, 2007; Freedman, 2010; Holliday Willey, 1999). Tasks must be divided and completed according to internal and external deadlines, and failure to do so for whatever reason (including misunderstanding the task, or feeling anxiety about completing it adequately) is likely to invoke the ire of others within the group. Thus it is incumbent upon the class teacher or tutor to be cognisant of any groups that may contain students on the spectrum who are likely to require a little more guidance than most of their counterparts. It may also be useful to provide information about tasks or assessments online or in other less traditional ways, in order to potentially facilitate earlier access and more time to consider what is expected and required.

When working with students with any kind of disability, we should be thinking in terms of Universal Design for Learning (UDL). Universal Design is the process of designing environments and products for all people, without the need for specialist design, and it has been proven to be more cost-effective than retrofitting when needed (Dell, Newton and Petroff, 2012). Additionally, other users also find benefits. Common examples include the standardised use of kerb cut-outs at road crossings, which allow wheelchair users to use the crossing, but have also proven useful for parents with prams and strollers, people with shopping trolleys, and mail delivery people who use carts to deliver mail in business districts. Similarly, closed captioning was originally designed to allow deaf viewers to enjoy television, but is now often used in noisy public areas, for those who are learning English (or another language), or by people trying to keep up with their favourite programme while their partner is sleeping! This is the idea that underpins such trends as wheelchair-accessible toilets being made available in all public buildings (including, in some countries, schools), even if there are currently no known users requiring such a facility. Within the education environment, however, we often manage the physical aspects of the learning environment – special access toilets and lifts are commonplace in universities – but may not do so well in terms of the delivery of the teaching materials. Universal Design for Learning combines these principles with brain research (Dell, Newton and Petroff, 2012). Universal Design for Learning is about providing the access and opportunity to both support and challenge students' learning needs (Hall and Stahl, 2006). It recognises that making material more easily accessible for a student with a disability will also make it more accessible for everyone. For example, reading aloud materials that are being transcribed from a brain storming activity may be instituted as a strategy to help a student with vision impairment, but it will also help students with Attention Deficit Hyperactivity Disorder (ADHD) who typically require multimodal instruction, as well as assisting their peers without disability who happen to be aural learners. Technology can be a useful tool, in that it 'can be universally beneficial for all students as a vehicle for learner engagement or conveyance of instructional content, and it can also promote participation, learning and performance by students with disabilities' (King-Sears, Swanson and Mainzer, 2011, p. 569).

Some individuals on the spectrum have bilateral coordination or grapho-motor difficulties, which make handwriting difficult. While traditionally we have viewed print as an effective, portable and convenient means of conveying information, for others it can create significant barriers (Hall and Stahl, 2006). These barriers are easily overcome by a willingness to also make materials available in digital form. Assistive technologies such as digital pens, laptops or tablets, and recording applications also provide simple and effective workarounds; each of which requires the knowledge and agreement of teaching staff because of privacy and copyright issues. When faced with such requests, be inclined to grant them; generally, if a student is better able to access learning materials, she or he will be better able to achieve to their potential.

Students on the spectrum often favour a computerised environment because it is predictable, consistent and more free from social demands (Golan and Baron-Cohen, 2006). But digital media and electronic texts offer opportunities to engage all students in learning (Dell, Newton and Petroff, 2012). The literature suggests that an online or virtual learning environment allows students with various learning needs to engage as and when they see fit in a socially acceptable manner. When learning and teaching materials are made available online, students who require large print, text-to-speech or easy reading/page decluttering software in order to access their materials more readily, are able to do so without being singled out as 'different' learners. Academics' fears that students may not attend physical lectures if the materials are made available online have not been supported by research, which suggests that only 1 per cent of students stop attending lectures for this reason (Newland, 2003). Indeed, our practice suggests that students with disabilities often seem to listen to lectures more than once, and typically will review or print out the slides beforehand, annotate them during the live lecture, and then listen to the lecture a second time when reviewing the materials – study strategies that must surely be recognised and supported as good practice.

The best way to reach a larger number of students, including those with disabilities, is to teach in a multimodal manner. In any classroom we will have students who are strongly kinaesthetic, strongly visual and strongly aural in terms of their learning modes, even before we consider Gardner's intelligences or any disabilities that might impede access to the information. For students on the spectrum, the aural mode of delivery is often particularly difficult –

and this is the mode most often used in the lecture/tutorial model favoured by universities and colleges.

Students on the spectrum will often do better with visual cues (Wagner, 2002). A number of students on the spectrum like university lectures better than high school classes, because they are often accompanied by lecture slides containing graphic representations of information. Marking rubrics, which are a good idea for all students, are particularly useful for helping this cohort to clearly perceive what is expected in class and in assessments (Wagner, 2009). Having a clear sense of that which the marker is seeking helps alleviate student anxiety (Wagner, 2009) – and also makes marking and feedback easier! Students who have been handed a grading chart are far less likely to query why they have been 'given' the awarded mark, since a concrete answer to that question has been provided.

People on the spectrum have often identified difficulty focusing on one person's voice when several are talking (Attwood, 1998), such as in a room with groups or one large group with more than one conversation taking place. This has implications for university groupwork that involves students on the spectrum. Our students have reported having difficulty knowing what to do or what is expected when a teacher breaks the large group into smaller groups, some stating that they feel stupid when they do something wrong or misunderstand the instructions. Challenges with auditory discrimination and distortion of speech can be reduced if the spoken instructions for what group members are required to do are also provided in the written mode – on the board or on handouts – as best practice in teaching.

## Attitudes and interventions

It may seem that the advice being offered here is creating an insurmountable list of things to add into an already crowded curriculum. For those who are casual academics, it will no doubt seem as though these are still more things that need to be thought about, organised and accommodated in your own time, since we all know that there is often a significant difference between the number of hours worked and the number of hours for which one is officially paid. The move towards a more inclusive curriculum, however, can be achieved incrementally, with strategies being employed as the need arises (Pearson and Koppi, 2006). Once you have implemented some strategies to better accommodate students on the spectrum, it is likely that you will continue to include them in your classroom practice and incrementally add to them, since improving teaching to accommodate students on the spectrum or with other disabilities almost inevitably leads to better teaching for all.

The key to many students on the spectrum learning is in having some flexibility – around setting, scheduling, timing, and methods of delivery and assessment – something for which the higher education sector is not typically known. Reasonable adjustments or accommodations around assessment are often the only areas in which there is any degree of flexibility at all, and these have been termed a 'necessary but insufficient solution' (Hall and Stahl, 2006, p. 74), since the recommended accommodations may not work efficiently for an individual student, yet the student is often reticent about explaining how or why it does not work for them, for fear that no further accommodations will be made, or being seen to 'complain' about the 'help' being offered. It may require an observant classroom teacher or member of the support staff to see that the adjustment needs to be altered in order to assist the student in a meaningful way.

From a teaching perspective, the only area over which you may have control is the method of delivery. In a lecture theatre or tutorial classroom, it is possible and, indeed, advisable to consider the multiple intelligences discussed in Chapter 2, and endeavour to deliver teaching materials in a multimodal manner in order for students with a range of learning profiles to be able to access the information. Traditional 'chalk-and-talk' lecturing, for example, really only services students who are strongly aural learners (those with high musical and linguistic intelligence). Supplementing teacher-directed lecturing with graphic representations on lecture slides, short video clips or online activities will allow students with differing learning profiles to engage with and understand the materials. Making teaching materials available in a digital form also allows the students to access them in different ways, both temporally (for pre-reading, or later revision) and logistically (since they are able to be used with assistive technologies such as text-to-speech software).

In terms of creating a supportive classroom atmosphere, it is important to not only have but also demonstrate patience and empathy. It may well be that the behaviour of the student on the spectrum is trying – but you must also be aware that it is not deliberate, and make some allowances while attempting to direct towards more socially appropriate behaviour.


### Eva

*Eva reported that she struggled to get out of bed in the morning. Consequently, she had a required campus timetable, and would only make appointments with Learning Development after 2.30 in the afternoon. No matter how many times I explained that my office hours ended at 4, or that I had children to collect, Eva could not empathise with this and would basically talk until she felt that she was finished.*

*Various strategies were employed, such as alarms on the mobile phone and computer, and organising for a colleague to call the phone on my desk. All to no avail – Eva would talk until the conversation was done, no matter how many messages I received or how distressed I became.*

*When Eva was experimenting with some subjects from Arts, she undertook a first-year philosophy class wherein she was learning about Emmanuel Kant's theories. One Friday afternoon a colleague stayed late, peering nervously through the blinds into my room. Eva insisted on using the 'proper' Germanic pronunciation of Kant. All my colleague could hear was a student shouting 'Kant! Kant!' increasingly loudly as she became more animated about the conversation. He was unsure*

> *whether to let it go, intervene, or call security, since he truly believed that I was being verbally abused by a student.*

Nola Norris unpacks this kind of scenario in her 2014 doctoral thesis, *A New Perspective on Thinking, Memory and Learning in Gifted Adults with Asperger Syndrome*. One of the adults she worked with for her dissertation found that she was not behaving appropriately in a courtroom situation, because she was shouting and waving her arms, which was interpreted as aggression. Once this was pointed out to her, she explained that she was unaware of the separation between spoken language and verbal thinking (Norris, 2014); the more strongly she believed something, the more loudly she articulated it. Similarly, Eva's passion for her Philosophy subject and her insistence on correct pronunciation led to a colleague believing that a faculty member was being called a pejorative term at significant volume. It was only because he could see that the person apparently being verbally abused was quite calm that he decided to wait and see what eventuated – and of course, nothing did, since this situation was not threatening, however it might have seemed. Understanding the context of the learner and offering some leeway saved Eva's enthusiasm from becoming a disciplinary incident.

## Codes of conduct for students

Students on the spectrum may be 'twice exceptional' – that is, they have the social disability of autism, coupled with being deemed gifted and/or talented. Autism Spectrum Disorder is not an intellectual disability, and some very intelligent people are on the spectrum; indeed, given the difficulty of completing compulsory education with a social disability like autism, it is arguably likely that it will be only the more determined and motivated students who attempt university straight away, and the best motivators for tertiary success are usually high intellect and a keen interest in a particular field. Generally speaking, university students with autism will have a clear, almost dogged, vocational reason for undertaking their studies (see Chapter 2); they are not typically found among the cohort who were unsure what to do post-school and so choose a generalist degree in order to buy more time to develop their interests. These students will require assistance with establishing the framework necessary to reach their potential.

One important but detrimental side-effect can be that the students develop an elitist attitude (Wagner, 2009) – one that unfortunately may be extended towards the teacher.

### Kenneth

*Kenneth seemed unable to reconcile that his long-developed views about the freedom of academic pursuits did not quite fit the reality of first-year, preliminary subjects. In a first-year English class, one of the prescribed texts was Oscar Wilde's* The Picture of Dorian Gray. *Where most students took to the text with some gusto, Kenneth appeared confused in class as to the direction of the conversation. He asked the tutor a question about one of Wilde's lovers, mispronouncing the name. The tutor deflected the comment and tried to bring Kenneth back to the discussion at hand, only to be faced with a student who was clearly furious and demanded to know how she dare to teach the class without a detailed knowledge of Wilde's intimate relationships, to which the puzzled teacher replied, 'because it's a class about the novel?'*

In this instance, clear expectations at the beginning of semester about the parameters for study – that is, which texts were to be examined each week, and in what context, as opposed to thesis-worthy attention to biographical detail – may have helped to avoid this situation. The student in question had not been flagged or even diagnosed as being on the spectrum, but this incident was part of a pattern of behaviour that suggested his social awkwardness may have been well beyond his control, or even understanding.

### Kenneth

*As part of the First-Year Experience (FYE), new students were encouraged to join the university team at an overnight community fundraising event held on a weekend early in the semester. Kenneth dutifully signed up. At the event, however, he did not participate in social or fundraising activities, instead ostentatiously reading a rather large book from the university library, and attempting to engage his tutor in a discussion about what he was reading as she packed up on Sunday morning. It was a university-organised event, and they were both there, therefore she was available. Ideas around boundaries, contexts, or even just the hours that casual staff are available went completely unexplored by Kenneth.*

Never assume students will pick up on cues (for example, that no one else is interrupting the professor mid-lecture in order to ask a question, so perhaps that is not a socially acceptable behaviour). There are some things that will need to be explained, even though they seem apparent to most people operating within the university environment. This needs to be done sensitively, however; although it is commonly believed that people on the spectrum do not have empathy, or, worse, do not have feelings, neither is true. Not knowing the socially acceptable way to express an emotion is not the same thing as not feeling it, and perhaps intensely. People on the spectrum may be sensitive and are often prone to anxiety and introversion; a combination almost tailor-made to have them replay an awkward or embarrassing situation in their heads, long after the moment has passed. You may, therefore, need to take the student aside quietly and explain that 'we don't do [unacceptable behaviour X] because [simple explanation Y] so we do [acceptable behaviour Z]'.

It is important that you check that the student has understood your intervention and explanation, so always have the student repeat to you what the required behaviour is and reach agreement on what future behaviour will be. For example, 'It's important not to interrupt me (the Professor) when I am lecturing because it breaks the flow of my prepared lecture and interrupts the thinking of other students. I would prefer that you raise any questions you might have during the time I have allowed for questions at the end of the lecture. Perhaps you could write a note of what your questions or comments are so that you can raise them at the end or raise them with your tutor. So, next time, what will you do in my lecture?' We would expect that the student would respond 'Next time I'll write down my questions and I'll raise them at the end of the lecture or with my tutor.' The vast majority of students who have successfully matriculated to university will have had some success in compulsory schooling and will therefore have had similar interventions in the past. Indeed, younger students may even have had the benefit of early intervention, unlike their older counterparts.

## Tips for Teachers

- Be wary of stereotyping and stigma. We teach students, not disabilities!

- Make sure your instructions are clear and concise, and, where possible, provide these in writing (on the board, in hard copy, or post them on the subject website) for all students.

- If teaching a 100 level class, it is likely that the majority of students will be new to the university, or new to that faculty. Take some time to describe what the classroom expectations are in your subject.

- Make sure students have been given enough time to process instructions or new information. Find opportunities to check their understanding. If you see that a student has misunderstood or is not participating as you require, then quietly speak with that student and re-iterate your instructions to clarify.

- Make sure students are clear about the consequences for non-attendance, non-compliance, non-preparation and non-submission.

- Be patient and try to understand the point of view of the student. Assume, at least in the first instance, that the goal of the student is not to make trouble, since it is more likely that she or he is merely misunderstanding cultural codes or classroom expectations.

- If a student constantly or inappropriately interrupts the class, try to ignore such interruptions and maintain focus on the central theme of the conversation. This is preferable to focusing on the interruption and asking the student what he or she means. To do so only prolongs the interruption, keeps discussion off track, and runs the risk of making the student feel stupid.

- Provide all students with good examples of academic writing that clearly demonstrate the written register required. If you have permission from the writer to do so, then consider posting appropriate examples on the subject website.

- If the student is engaging in unusual behaviour, such as lying on the floor, invite the student to sit with the group. If it occurs again, repeat the invitation and also request the student speaks with you at the end of class. Make it clear what behaviour is unacceptable and describe what behaviour is acceptable.

- In the case of sexual innuendo or other inappropriate references, it is important to stop the behaviour before it gathers any momentum. If it has occurred within a classroom, then an immediate statement to the effect that this is not acceptable behaviour is the best course of action. Solving the situation will be simplest if it involves a direct intervention by you. Follow up after the class by discussing the unwanted behaviour (or language) with the student and suggesting alternative and appropriate ways to behave.

- Check that the student has understood your intervention and explanation. Perhaps have the student repeat to you what the required behaviour is and reach agreement on what future behaviour will be.

## Tips for Learners

- Make sure you are clear about the consequences for non-attendance, non-compliance, non-preparation and non-submission. Unlike in high school, you do not progress within the degree if you do not attend and submit assessment tasks on time or sit the examinations.

- Make sure you check the subject website regularly to receive any amended or updated instructions.

- Read this chapter to find out the differences between the kinds of classes you will be attending (lectures, tutorials, seminars, workshops, laboratories).

- Understand that all learning situations have an established level of formality that is appropriate, such as lectures requiring the audience to remain silent unless invited to participate; and tutorials requiring student participation, but within particular frameworks, such as discussing a topic after or during a student presentation, as outlined by the tutor.

- It is never appropriate to become overly familiar with your lecturer or tutor, including it is never appropriate to write emails that are chatty or personally familiar. This is a workplace, so emails should be professional in tone.

- Be patient and try to understand the point of view of the teacher and other students. If you misunderstand the classroom expectations, ask the tutor to repeat any instructions or requirements so that you are clear.

- Follow the behaviour of the other students as a guide for your own. If they are asking questions, then it is OK for you to ask questions too. If they are not asking questions, then it is unlikely that you should do so at that time. If other students are sitting down, then you should too.

- If the class has not started yet and other students are talking together, then it is likely to be a private conversation and joining in may not be welcome.

- If the class has started and students are talking in groups, then you should be in a group too. Ask the tutor which group you should join.

- In a classroom tutorial, if the tutor or another student is giving a presentation (speaking), then you should not interrupt until invited to do so.

- Try to modulate your voice and tone. There is not, for most people, a direct correlation between certainty and volume. This means that you should use a calm speaking voice when participating in class (similar to what people use in shops or at the bank), not a loud voice.

# Chapter 4

# Rigidity of Thinking and Literal Thinking

## Introduction

Autism Spectrum Disorder is often marked by literal, rigid and pedantic thinking. This may cause problems both in classroom environments and at assessment time. In response to surveys of employers, which have ranked highly the capacity for new graduates to participate effectively as work team members, colleges and universities have introduced mandatory groupwork as part of most, if not all, subjects within each discipline as a means of developing team skills. Increasingly, college and university courses are utilising groupwork as a means of ensuring graduates are work-ready in this regard. They are also beginning to use more creative forms of assessment in an attempt to expand students' horizons. For students on the spectrum, the variety of skills that need to be internalised in order to complete these assessment tasks must seem like an ever-increasing list designed specifically to create uncertainty and anxiety. Just when they are learning how to write a quality university-level essay, they are asked to write a personal reflection, a report or group report, a blog, provide a 'digital artefact', or create a poster or a booklet! This can lead to 'Foolish

Jack' Syndrome, where, like the character from the fable, one set of skills and strategies is applied to a learning task or assignment for which they are inappropriate.

Understanding the demands of particular assessment tasks can also be very challenging. In the tertiary environment, much of the curriculum is hidden and assignment instructions can be opaque. Lorraine Wolf, Jane Thierfeld Brown and Ruth Kukiela Bork, in their excellent guide for college professionals, note that, '[t]rouble can crop up in one or several aspects of the writing process, including content, parameters of the assignment, focus and structure' (Wolf, Thierfeld Brown and Kukiela Bork, 2009, p. 42). They identify significant assessment challenges around such tasks as: plot analysis or character motivation; comparing and contrasting; personal, reflective tasks and analytical essays, in particular (Wolf, Thierfeld Brown and Kukiela Bork, 2009). They also identify problems around meta-tasks, such as understanding essay questions and expectations, planning, time management and the focus of papers, and initiating and sustaining long-term assignments; areas to which we return in Chapter 5.

In this chapter, we examine the ways in which the inflexible thinking patterns typical of those with Autism Spectrum Disorder can be a hindrance, as well as suggest some simple strategies for accommodating this. It can be difficult to persuade a neurotypical student of the nuances between a scholarly, reflective piece and personal opinion, polemic or editorialising; or between a report and an essay. The difficulties are compounded for students on the spectrum who think rigidly. For this cohort, unlearning a process, or knowing that it needs to be applied selectively, often appears to be more difficult than the process of learning to develop and apply the steps in the first place.

## Rigidity of thinking

Sometimes a student on the spectrum may be so rigid in his or her thinking as to characterise the undesirable or unfamiliar assignments as 'stupid', and may resist engaging with them altogether in the hope that protesting the pointlessness of the assignment may lead to it being changed. This is, of course, a particularly short-sighted strategy, since the likelihood of the assessment changing is even more remote than the likelihood of shifting the student's thinking on the topic.

## Jackson

*Jackson was a twenty-something young man who was referred for Learning Development assistance because he was not doing as well as he had hoped in his Education studies. With his first professional experience looming, his lecturers were concerned about his suitability for the programme (see Chapter 1), and Jackson was concerned that he was receiving marks below what he had reasonably expected, based on his high school performance. He brought with him the assignment on which he was working, which he deemed to be 'stupid'. The assignment required students to use postmodernist ideas to demonstrate ideas about there being multiple ways of knowing – and therefore multiple ways of learning and teaching. According to Jackson, there were not multiple ways of knowing: facts are facts, and students should learn facts, and there was nothing else to know.*

*I dutifully (and, arguably, inadvisedly) used an everyday example I had previously used with great success in classroom situations to explain the concept of 'multiple realities'. I talked about the instances where you see eyewitnesses on the news, describing car accidents. I suggested that if three of us were to witness a car accident outside the building, that we would all say similar things, but likely with slightly different accounts, or a slightly different focus on particular details. All three accounts, I argued, would be 'true', because they were very true for that individual; but it would be hard to argue that any one of those recounts was the truth. Jackson rejected this idea out of hand. He threw his pencil across the desk in disgust. 'There is one truth,' he insisted; 'it's whatever the police officer on duty decides happened.'*

*As I tried to point out that that was merely one person's best assessment of the alternative truths and perhaps there was not one defined, linear absolute, he became increasingly physically agitated; closing his eyes,*

> *jerking his knee up and down and generally appearing as though he was*
> *battling to contain a violent physical rage. He left the office not only still*
> *convinced that the assignment was stupid, but now seemingly convinced*
> *that I was, too.*

In instances like this, it is better to avoid engaging in an argument about the relative worth – or otherwise – of the set task. Instead, use *partial agreement*. A favourite of schoolteachers and parents, this strategy can be used to effectively stop the most circular of arguments. A typical school playground interaction using partial agreement would be around asking a student to pick up nearby rubbish. Inevitably, the student's first response is something along the lines of 'I didn't drop it' or 'it's not mine'. Rather than getting into a debate about who dropped it, when or why, it is more productive to say, 'That's probably true. But I'd still like you to pick it up.' Similarly, when an adult learner is arguing about the uselessness of a required academic task, it may be more productive to say, 'You may be right, but the assignment is not going to change, so we need to work out the best way of approaching it.' A helpful approach with a student like Jackson is to lessen his frustration by acknowledging how he is feeling. Instead of trying to explain postmodern thought using the eyewitness example, I could have said, 'I know this can be hard to accept. We grow up thinking that there is just one reality, but sometimes we really believe something to be true, and others really believe the exact opposite. It can be hard to prove who is right. In this assignment, you really need to outline ways of teaching and knowing based on different belief systems.' It is likely that Jackson would have also needed assistance in brainstorming what those different ways of knowing might be, in order to generate some search terms so that he could complete the assignment.

Once the student has agreed to engage with the assignment, the next step is interpreting its requirements. Individuals on the spectrum are often characterised as 'being very black and white' in their views, and these binary modes of thinking can be problematic when it comes to assessment. Even though a student is actively seeking advice from a university-based professional, the student may often have preconceived ideas about how she or he will approach a particular learning or assessment task. In some cases, it can be difficult to shift the student's thinking to be more in line with what the academic marker might be expecting to see.

## Learning cultures and rigidity of thinking

Formal learning occurs across a wide range of situations and within a variety of institutions: universities and colleges; technical, technological and vocational institutions; high schools and elementary or primary schools; and within the workplace. Brigid Ballard and John Clanchy have provided a useful way of understanding the various approaches to teaching and learning that exist within this range of situations, or 'learning cultures'. They suggest there are three broad learning cultures that incorporate distinct teaching and learning strategies: these are 'reproductive', 'analytic' and 'speculative' learning cultures. The aims of a reproductive learning culture are largely 'correctness' and the 'simple ("unreconstructed") transfer of knowledge and skills' (Ballard and Clanchy, 1991, p. 13). In this learning culture, the role of the teacher is the almost exclusive source of knowledge, providing direction and guidance and undertaking assessment. The characteristic teaching activities are the transmission of information, and learning is measured by demonstration of skills and assessment. These are geared to ranking, emphasising replication and testing memory recall and practical demonstration of skills learned, through activities that involve summarising, describing, identifying and applying formulae and information in answer to characteristic questions that focus on answering 'What?'

Reproductive learning cultures are typical within the school system, although there has been a shift in recent years toward the inclusion of higher-order thinking skills, such as analysis, evaluation, and synthesis (Anderson, Krathwohl and Bloom, 2001). Undergraduate and postgraduate coursework students in universities and colleges, however, are largely required to operate within an analytic learning culture, the aim of which is to develop independent and critical styles of thinking and the capacity for theory and abstraction. Students are required to demonstrate '"simple" originality [by] reshaping [research] material into a different pattern' (Ballard and Clanchy, 1991, p. 13) through the completion of written assignments, particularly essays and reports. Assessments require critical analysis and problem solving, with grades resting on the 'quality of interpretation' (Ballard and Clanchy, 1991, p. 13). The role of the teacher includes being a critical guide and questioner, pushing students towards higher-order thinking by asking 'why? how? how valid? how important?' (Ballard and Clanchy, 1991, p. 13), 'do you believe?' and 'to what extent?' The characteristic activities of an analytic learning culture are the analysis of information and ideas within interpretive frameworks and the modelling of critical approaches to knowledge and academic conventions.

Postgraduate research degrees are undertaken within a speculative learning culture, where the role of the teacher is that of a 'more experienced colleague and collaborator, a preliminary critic and advisor or patron' (Ballard and Clanchy, 1991, p. 13). The aim of speculative learning is the 'development of speculative, critical intelligence and expansion of [the] knowledge base (theory, data techniques)' through independent research and the completion of a thesis or dissertation of publishable quality that makes a 'contribution to the field of knowledge'. Students on the spectrum often demonstrate rigidity in moving beyond reproductive learning to analytic learning, preferring to demonstrate what they have learned through tests of recall, rather than tests that assess their 'ability to make abstractions and apply these to a range of real world scenarios' or 'those that involve a process of synthesis and development of new knowledge' (Gluck and Draisma, 1997, p. 8). When the teaching, learning and assessment activities undertaken in a university or college course differ from those previously experienced by a student on the spectrum, typically the student will rigidly adhere to past strategies, often failing to interpret the overt as well as the hidden curriculum, and thus failing to meet the assessment criteria.

The following case study elucidates the problem of rigidity of thinking and the inability to make adjustments between one learning culture and another. It also shows how failure to understand the different roles of teacher (exclusive source of knowledge, direction and guidance versus questioner and critical guide) and that of learner (dependent versus independent) manifest in the transition from one learning context to another. At the time, however, the student's primary focus was on the logistical issues of getting to university rather than operating functionally as a university student once he was actually on campus.

### Tom

*Tom is a student from a regional area who has long had social difficulties. By about the second to last year of primary school, he had become a school refuser. With the support of understanding parents, he eventually completed his high school studies via distance education and enrolled in a local technical and vocational college where he undertook a computer programming course. He did well enough in this course to matriculate to a major university a little over an hour away, and received a scholarship, based on high achievement in the college course, in the process. Tom and his family did all the right things with regard to his transition; visiting the university, registering with Disability Services, undertaking tours, and making sure that he was referred for academic help.*

*The first major hurdle we faced was with making appointments in the first place. Tom could not have early appointments, because he is often tired and less functional in the mornings. Nor could he stay late, because he felt it would be unsafe to walk home from the railway station in the dark. He struggled to find times that he felt suited his train and bus timetables. He articulated, in fine detail, every nuance of his train and bus timetable, to the point of social inappropriateness. I finally suggested that I could give him a lift, given that I would be travelling up from the same area on the day in question. Tom said that he could not travel by car because he suffers from car sickness. In the end, he decided to make an appointment for which he knew he would be running late, because of the late bus connection.*

*At Tom's first appointment, the most standout features were its brevity, and Tom's complete lack of affect. Tom rightly believed himself to have already been an excellent student in a post-school educational environment. When I, as his Learning Development Lecturer, tried to work with him to create a plan for his learning, teaching and assessment, Tom rejected some parts of it outright; arguing, for example, that he did not need help writing essays. At his second appointment, we discussed a reflective writing piece. Tom really could not understand why reflection was relevant, and did not appear to be really taking in the advice on hand, saying that he knew what he needed to do, but with his body language suggesting that he very much resented having to do it. He also insisted that he needed to leave the appointment early, because he had a group assignment to work on, and his travel restrictions meant that his group mates could only meet at a time that clashed, in part, with our booked appointment. Given all of this, I reminded Tom that he could make an appointment with me at any time, but sent him on his way.*

*Tom did not make a further appointment, but evidently sent a panicky email to his Disability Liaison Officer the weekend after he received his first set of marks. Feedback from the marker indicated that he was on the wrong track for the next piece of scaffolded work: the reflection, due on Monday.*

The frustration when students reject advice is immense – on both sides. The student has been seeking help that they know they need, yet since it has not taken the form expected and therefore does not fit the established world view, it must be wrong. The student thus leaves convinced that help was requested but not received. Equally, the staff member may well be able to see exactly what it is that the student needs to do differently in order to demonstrate to a marker the extent of their knowledge, but if the student refuses to receive or implement that advice, there is little to do but sit back and watch the predictable consequences come to fruition, and be ready to attempt to help when – and if – the student asks again.

### Tom

*Tom was persuaded to return. This time, the Learning Development Lecturer made it clear that Tom was expected to stay for the entire consultation, since learning how to do assessments is just as important as doing them.*

*Visual scaffolding was used to demonstrate to Tom the elements typically expected in a reflective piece. Sequencing ideas in boxes can often help students to focus on a smaller and more manageable target.*

| Step 1: | Step 2: | Step 3: | Step 4: |
|---|---|---|---|
| What do you already know/ feel about the topic? | Complete set readings about the topic. Make note of details, as well as anything that challenged your preconceived ideas, anything that was new to you, or anything that surprised you or made you alter your thinking a little. Make note of why/how it impacted. | Write up the assignment. | Go back through the assignment and see if there are comments throughout about how your thinking/ actions changed/ were adjusted, where and why. Add in these parts (your reflection), if they are missing. |

In some cases, more scaffolding might be needed. Consider allocating word targets to each section (for example, '250 words on X') or giving samples of well-integrated reflective comments.

Part of the issue for Tom lay in the fact that he was not only transitioning from one type of learning to another, but from one level (technical and vocational education) to another (university/ college). Points of transition can be difficult, especially if the student has had some success in the previous environment; the strategies learned and employed worked previously, so they will be rigidly applied to the new context. Most of us would understand that even if we have successfully completed an undergraduate degree, the expectations at postgraduate level may be higher and require us to put in more effort in order to meet the new (but largely unspoken) standards. A student on the spectrum, however, may rationalise that the amount of effort that was used when previously at university or college was adequate, and therefore that is how much effort is required for *all* tertiary courses.

## Types of learning and conditions for learning

Students may have long-held beliefs about what constitutes learning and assessment and inappropriately apply these from one situation to another. Most people understand that 'learning' involves increasing 'what', or 'how much', the learner knows and are very familiar with situations that test how much has been learned. These tests usually seek to determine what has been remembered or what can be reproduced and to rank learners in terms of achievement. Another type of learning situation is one that is geared to establishing competence and, eventually, proficiency, and entails the acquisition of facts, skills and methods through practice. What separates university education from these other types is that it focuses on higher-order thinking skills rather than simply focusing on remembering and reproducing what has been learned. Instead, university learning provides experiences for students that require deduction and abstraction of meaning and the establishment of relationships between parts of subject matter and real situations. It also pushes students toward hypothesising and theorising and testing these against reality in a process that involves whether learners can question and reframe knowledge through a process of synthesis and development of new knowledge (Gluck and Draisma, 1997).

In Tom's case, he wrongly anticipated that the kind of learning he undertook in a vocational institution would be appropriate for a university, and that the time allocated in order to succeed would be similar.

### Tom

*Tom struggled to understand the information that was being aurally conveyed in his lectures and tutorials. When I suggested that we look at some note-taking strategies and/or technologies, however, he refused to engage, saying that he believed that he was getting all the required information from research, and that he was comfortable with that mode of learning because he had used it for distance education and at TAFE and done well.*

*Tom had not adjusted the time he allocated to study, however, despite the fact that the academic expectations were higher; that the readings were lexically dense; that – by his own admission – he needed a lot of time to read and digest information; and that he was needing to spend hours on additional readings to compensate for the one-hour lectures that his peers were using to gain basic information, but he still needed time to do the additional readings and research required for his assignments. This would have contributed, in part, to the panicked email sent to his Disability Liaison Officer the night before the reflection was due.*

Given the difficulty of attempting to navigate a neurotypical world when one is on the spectrum, it is perhaps unsurprising that those with autistic traits will return to thought patterns that they find are more comfortable, or with which they have had success in the past. This is not to say that they cannot learn, however; Thomas Armstrong and others (Armstrong, 2010; Doige, 2007; Eagleman, 2011; Merzenich, 2013) argue for the neuroplasticity of the brain. Huttenlocher suggests that the brain has remarkable plasticity and this allows a damaged part to be taken over by another (Huttenlocher, 1984).

Cambourne and Turbill have established the ideal conditions for learning (Cambourne and Turbill, 1987), which we have seen lead to successful learning outcomes in a variety of learners (Gluck and Draisma, 1997), including those on the spectrum. Cambourne and Turbill list the 'Conditions of Learning' as immersion, demonstration, expectations, responsibility, approximation, practice, engagement and response (Cambourne and Turbill, 1987).

*Immersion* involves the student being 'immersed' in the medium of the university culture, at the macro level, and in the discipline and subjects in which she or he is enrolled, at the micro level. It occurs naturally in lectures, tutorials and other classroom experiences and it occurs when students are exposed to the range of reading materials for their subjects and research. *Demonstration(s)* of the discipline-specific requirements occurs during the immersion process and throughout the subject. The *expectations* 'given off', verbally and non-verbally by teaching staff, are that all students will succeed, and that they are expected to take *responsibility* for their own learning, since university is an adult learning environment. *Approximation*, or the franchise 'to have a go', occurs when students participate in tutorials, seminars, laboratories and other practical classes, where their attempts to solve problems or discuss issues are authentic and where informal and formal feedback serves to moderate or confirm their thinking. Approximation also occurs when students submit written assessments, such as essays, reports and the like, and receive feedback *responses* from their markers, or from fellow students. Regular participation in the classroom provides students with opportunities for authentic *practice* in employing and developing their thinking. From the time they enrol in a subject, students are engaged in the process of doing academic tasks and this *engagement* with the demonstrations that are made available, as well as the mutual exchanges between experts and novices that occur throughout the process, facilitate learning (Gluck and Draisma, 1997).

## Communication difficulties

Once appropriate study patterns are established and students are engaged with learning, there may still be communication difficulties. Instruction based on conceptual knowledge may involve understanding multiple representations of information, attempting to think about or explain how or why something works, draw attention to more than one solution method, or apply one's own understanding to generate solutions (Foreman and Arthur-Kelly, 2014). All of these processes are cognitively demanding, and are extremely difficult for students with working memory and lateral thinking issues. There is also an ethical obligation to help students succeed in their studies. Try to place yourself in the position of the students and remember which things you had to work out for yourself when you were newly enrolled. Explaining these things clearly will help all students, and will likely lead to better results and a far less painful marking process. It is always best practice to give instructions in a multimodal format; although telling students what to do may work for some of them, writing instructions down as well as describing what is required is likely to work for *most* students in your classroom.

People on the Autism Spectrum sometimes have problems interpreting metaphorical language, and as Catherine Wearing argues, the central difference between literal and metaphorical cases lies in the ability to draw on sources that help with the interpretive process (Wearing, 2010). In literal examples, the required information can be found within the realms of science and real world knowledge; in metaphorical examples, the listener must be able to decode which features are being used as representative aspects. It is perhaps unsurprising, then, that students on the spectrum have issues when interpreting assignment requirements or the hidden curriculum since these, too, require drawing on abstract understandings.

As teachers of academic skills, when students tell us they 'just can't write essays', we often use the analogy of baking a cake: that if you follow the structure – the recipe – and include all the right elements – the ingredients – what you end up with will end up looking pretty much as it should and performing its primary function. But some people are naturally good essay writers in the same way that some bakers have a particularly light touch – others will have cakes that cave in in the middle, and, in much the same way, some essays will be a little messy but nevertheless have the overall shape that they should (McMahon-Coleman, 2015). Unfortunately, a similar analogy had evidently been adopted by one of the tutors in the one of the schools at our institution, who helpfully made and illustrated an information sheet to this effect to go along with the set essay question. The first we knew of this was when one of our students on the spectrum turned up at Learning Development with an essay question, the 'tip' sheet and a very confused look on his face.

### James

*James had an essay question that required him to respond in terms of explaining an art theory, discussing the work of a related practitioner, and then adding a reflective viewpoint in each paragraph. The tip sheet used the metaphor of a layer cake, with theory/practitioner/reflection as layers that were to be repeated in order. James asked in horror, 'do I have to bake a cake?' Even when advised that this was not the case, he continued to wave the tip sheet as evidence that he did. He struggled to be convinced that the tip sheet was tangential to the main task and a metaphoric way of providing advice, instead; since it was something concrete and provided by the tutor, he reasoned that it must be critical.*

The use of metaphoric language is not the only area where there are issues involving interpretation. There may also be problems around concepts and terminology in the learning activities and assessments. Just as students on the spectrum may be unfamiliar with metaphorical language, they may sometimes have issues adjusting to synonyms for information already learned. Umbrella terms such as 'assignment' or 'assessment task' can sometimes be conflated with more specific genre types, such as 'report' or 'essay', even though they lack specificity. When a student researches those terms, it can become confusing. One can only imagine the chaos that would be the result of posing the question 'how do I write an assignment' into a search engine, which is a likely scenario for students who struggle with decoding language and finding appropriate synonyms. If 'assignment' is used interchangeably with a more specific genre of assignment such as a 'report', which in various academic disciplines adopts a quite specific form, further confusion may result. Similarly, the word 'essay' in some sub-disciplines (English Literature, History, Philosophy, for example) of the liberal Arts is typically interpreted to mean one cogent argument without sub-headings, tables or illustrations. In other sub-disciplines of Arts or in the discipline of Social Sciences (Creative Arts, Education, Human Geography, Psychology, Sociology, Economics) the term 'essay' *requires* the inclusion of sub-headings, tables and illustrations, and the lack of those genre markers would inevitably lead to a loss of marks. Worse, we have on occasion found instances where subject or course outlines referred to an assessment as an essay in the title, but proceeded to invite students to write a report in the more detailed instructions. As teachers, therefore, we need to be confident that our specific expectations about the assignments we set and the genre we require have been thoroughly made explicit to all students.

## Assignment genre

### Essay

An essay is a structured argument about a particular topic. It will contain a thesis/argument throughout that addresses a set question and will require critical material and/or primary materials to support the points made. In Arts/Liberal Arts/Humanities subject areas, an essay usually requires that there be no sub-headings or visual support material, including tables; however, in faculties such as Law or Social Sciences (for example, Education, Sociology, Psychology) these genre differences are not only tolerated, but required.

## Plan or essay schemata

Sometimes lecturers will set a plan or schemata as a scaffolded learning activity prior to submission of a major essay. The advantage of this is that students receive some feedback on their arguments and how they intend to present them before putting them together for what is often a significant proportion of their course mark. This will be anathema, however, to those students who like to 'write their way into a topic' and find pre-planning to be an extremely difficult task indeed. Students on the spectrum who also fall into this category will need to be reassured that plans are adaptable and can – and should – be changed if marker feedback suggests that the intended path is not optimal.

## Report

A report is similar to an essay in content and tone, but is typically organised under designated headings and sub-headings. These may vary according to the discipline – for example, a scientific report will look quite different from a company report in a Business subject. Students may need to be taught some of the counter-intuitive aspects of report writing (for example, that the short abstract that comes at the very beginning of a report is typically written last).

## Book report

This may seem like something students know how to do, but the requirements will obviously differ from what they were in primary school! A university-level book report will typically not only summarise the plot, but will move beyond that to discuss key themes or issues, as well as any 'silences' (for example, are women's voices heard in the text? Or Indigenous voices?). It may also include some preliminary critical commentary, since reading the critical responses of others often offers insight. In Social Science faculties, a book report or a similar report on a journal article will often require the student to focus on the research topic that is the subject of the book or article, making comments about the rationale for the research, the methodology and methods of research, and the validity and perhaps transferability of the results.

## Tutorial presentation (with or without PowerPoint or similar) and/or tutorial paper

Tutorial presentations involve summarising a particular text or topic, including some critical commentary, and pointing out the strengths or limitations of approaches to that topic. Very often, there is a written component as well, and these are usually due the week *after* the presentation. The idea behind this is that any ideas or debate that arose in class after the presentation can be included in the write-up. Despite this, it is surprising how many students hand in the exact transcript from their presentation, with no editing or amendments. Some disciplines expect that a tutorial paper will be in the form of an essay; others, that it will be in the form of a report or a summary. Make your expectations clear to the students in your classes.

## Reflection

Reflective pieces can be confronting for all students, but particularly for those on the spectrum. The idea of reflective practice popularised by Donald Schon (Schon, 1983) focused on reflecting *in* practice (while doing it) and *on* practice (after doing it). Some assessment tasks require students to write a 'Reflective Diary' throughout the semester, commenting on theory that has been read or discussed in class and on the relationship between theory and any practical experience gained in the subject (such as in Education, Nursing, Medicine, Law, Sport Science, Psychology). When students are asked to do reflection, markers are typically expecting to see not only a summary of what they did, but some insight into how they felt about it or how their thinking has been changed or modified as a result. This obviously can be difficult for literal rigid thinkers who are change-resistant.

## Wiki posts

Wiki posts are posts made in an online forum and are designed to be informative (as per Wikipedia). Theoretically, they should be able to be edited by others, but few online teaching platforms seem to have this capability.

## Blog posts

Blog posts are similar to Wiki posts, but typically are less factual and more in the realm of opinion writing. Many subjects with online discussion spaces now ask students to blog or contribute to online discussion as part of their participation and assessment within courses.

## Blog

In some disciplines (such as Information and Communication Technologies or Journalism), students may be asked to establish an entire blog, not just with posts, but 'Contact' and 'About us' pages and so on. These will typically be open access, using hosts such as *WordPress*.

## Commentary

Similar to a book report, students may be asked to complete a reading and critique it for its strengths and limitations.

## Poster

Students may be well aware of decorative posters, but within the university context, posters are more like the primary school assignments completed on cardboard! They are a visual representation of the most important points. Selection of visual images is therefore as important as the content and references. While there are specialist software programs available, merely arranging the information on a single PowerPoint slide and printing it to A3 size is likely the easiest solution.

## Brochure/booklet

Again, there are specialist software programs, but using the 'Booklet' template within Word may prove to be the easiest option. As with posters, the inclusion and clear layout of information is important.

## Groupwork

Groupwork may be structured (with assigned roles) or unstructured (where it is up to the members to decide who will do which tasks). Most times, they are marked as a group activity so that everyone gets the same mark, but increasingly this is being modified to a hybrid model where a portion of the marks are awarded to the individual student (often based on a reflective piece of writing on how the activity went). This is designed to promote fairness and assuage students who worry about being 'marked down' because of a 'lazy' group member, or who end up doing more than their fair share in order to not be penalised. Of course, for students on the spectrum who find reflective writing difficult, this strategy will not necessarily lead to improved marks!

## Role play

Almost universally loathed by students, role plays are sometimes used in language classes, drama classes, journalism classes and education classes. Moot court activities in Law are also essentially structured role plays. These are favoured by teaching staff because they give students an opportunity to apply the skills they are learning.

## Model

Scale models may be required in some Engineering subjects. Models are also used in problem-based learning in Engineering, Architecture, Building Science and Physics.

### Lesson plan/unit plan/teaching resources

All typically used in Education, there are subtle differences between these. Lesson plans are used to programme a particular class or activity; unit plans are the broader plan for a number of weeks, into which the lesson plan fits. Teaching resources are worksheets, games, activities, apps and so on that are used within those lessons. Unit and lesson plan proformas are readily available online. Typically, student-teachers would need to think about: what they want to teach, how they will teach it, how they will know if the students have learned what they taught, and how that lesson fits in to the sequence of other lessons within the unit.

### Micro-teaching or micro-practice

Micro-teaching is what it sounds like: small-scale teaching. It is often used in Education, but micro-practice may also be used elsewhere, such as in Nursing (teaching another to take and record blood pressure), Mathematics (teaching others to use a particular method) or in Sport Science or Medicine (learning to take a history or practise on patients). Students demonstrate their understanding of a concept by teaching it to their peers.

Confusion can even occur around the use of discipline-specific vocabulary. An example we have used to explain to students the importance of understanding terminology within the context of the discipline is the use of the word 'character'. For a student of English Literature, Cultural Studies or Film, 'character' means a person portrayed in a novel, short story, play, poem, on film or in television. For a student of Psychology, however, 'character' can occasionally be used synonymously with 'personality'; in Philosophy it can mean a person's ethical or moral stance; in Computing Science it can mean a blip on the screen; in Japanese or Chinese, it can mean a pictogram.

### Edward

*Edward came to visit Learning Development with an assignment for BioMedical Science that he was finding tricky. The question contained the phrase 'Anaphylaxis', which he had dutifully looked up, and for which he had written a definition. When the Learning Development Lecturer used the phrase, 'anaphylactic shock', however, Edward became frustrated and upset, insisting that the question was not about anaphylactic shock; it was about anaphylaxis.*

It is important when teaching to use the various forms of terms or synonyms for terms in order to expand students' academic vocabularies within the discipline and to provide them with terminology that they will come across in their research readings. For example, when using the noun form, 'anaphylaxis', it would have been helpful if Edward's lecturer had also used the common adjectival form 'anaphylactic shock'. Synonyms and expanded terms serve to do this for all students and, importantly, provide the student with Autism Spectrum Disorder with a broader and easier point of entry into the subject matter being discussed. This is not to suggest that pre-learning vocabulary will solve all problems, however; as Richard Lavoie demonstrates, vocabulary without context will still prove opaque to some learners (Lavoie, 1989). Indeed, this was what Tom was finding when he was attending the lectures but not comprehending them, and so returning home to conduct his own research into the topics that had been discussed in class.

The nuances of social conversation are also problematic, and we are often unaware of the number of phrases we use on a daily basis that require an understanding of subtext. As teachers, we tend to move straight to, 'it's kind of like – ' analogies in order to help a puzzled-looking student. We are also typically quite proficient users of language, who are well aware of idiom, cliché and adage. Students on the spectrum may not share this knowledge.

### Donna

*Donna was referred to Learning Development by her counsellor, who felt she might need help decoding assignment requirements. Donna dutifully made an appointment, turned up to it, and engaged in the process. At the end of the appointment, having discussed her learning needs at great length, I opened my diary and said, 'So, I'll see you again – ?'*

*'Oh, I don't think so,' she replied.*

*She had been referred to see me, and she had seen me. (McMahon-Coleman, 2015)*

People on the Autism Spectrum are typically very rule bound and, as teachers, we can use this to our advantage. While students on the spectrum may not intuit what the rules or parameters for behaviour are, once they are established, they will tend to follow them religiously – for example, to the point of insisting to the fire warden stopping everyone from entering the building with alarms blaring that they have a tutorial in that building, and must enter in order not to be late! In the case above, the feedback report to the referring body noted the above conversation. Donna's counsellor was very experienced in dealing with students on the spectrum, and responded in a manner designed to encourage her to re-engage with the process.

### Donna

*When next he spoke with Donna, her counsellor told her that she had to see Learning Development several times during the semester – which was not, technically speaking, true (McMahon-Coleman, 2015). He nominated to her the exact number of visits that I had recommended in my feedback to him, after the initial consultation. Donna attended every one of her appointments and a useful teaching programme was put in place. On one memorable occasion, half the appointment became about me struggling to explain the phrase, 'can't see the wood for the trees' that I had used.*

*Donna graduated at the same time as the rest of her cohort. Contrary to her suggestion after her first meeting that she would never see me again, she has remained in touch since graduation, and has even come to the office to say hello when she has been in town visiting family. She did, however, routinely write on my evaluation forms that I 'used too many metaphors!'*

It is very rare to find a university discipline that does not require students to communicate in some form. Indeed, even in Computing Science classes, students are now often asked to complete group oral presentations as a means of improving graduates' abilities to listen, understand, and respond to a client's brief. In recent years, we have been asked by faculty members to give workshops to classes of Information and Communication Technologies (ICT) students in order to enable them to be able to engage in effective conversations within assessment tasks and beyond. Yet, even in its most pure form, Computer Sciences – long perceived as a discipline wherein introverts could avoid real-life communication – in fact centres on the effective transfer of information. Misunderstandings occur in coding when those writing code and those using the program have different interpretations of the same action, and these can have profound consequences for end users.

It is an unfortunate reality that, given class sizes and the largely autonomous adult-learning environment, we may not notice that particular students are in trouble until very late in the piece. Unfortunately, neither might they. In the case of Tom (see page 101), he was both unaware that he was heading down a tangent and unwilling to listen to advice to that effect, leaving him at crisis point the weekend before an assignment was due. Rachel (introduced in Chapter 2) was another case in point. She not only started things late, she had problems around being organised on a daily basis. It was not until she was repeating – and failing – the final three subjects in her course that she was referred for assistance, as she had appeared to be coping until that very late stage.

## Rachel

*Rachel was easily distracted by tangents during our initial consultation. She made an appointment several weeks after she was referred, when the semester was half over. She maintained that her problem was with remembering formulae for examinations. She would not canvass discussing any other study or time-management strategies that were not directly related. Her referral documentation showed that her faculty adviser had recommended that she seek counselling to try to unravel why she had suddenly hit such a road block in her studies. Rachel would not consider this option in our discussion, either; she did not have problems with exam anxiety, she said, just with recalling formulae in exams. We discussed some strategies for improving her recall, and I showed her some flashcards I had made. I encouraged her to come and see me again and let me know how she was going, and show me her revision flashcards. I thought that I had made it clear that she was to do this prior to her exams. About a month later, Rachel emailed me one Sunday and asked could I help her locate assessment information she'd been directed to by her lecturer at the beginning of the semester, but couldn't find. Could I look for it before she came to see me on Monday, she asked. The information was easily located, and revealed that she would need to submit her capstone project in three weeks' time – even though it was supposed to represent three months' work and it was apparent from her email that, despite her earlier good intentions, she had not started it.*

*At this point, I checked my diary and discovered that while Rachel might be intending to stop by on Monday, she was not one of the students who had actually booked an appointment that afternoon. When I pointed this out, she replied that she didn't need to make an appointment, because I'd said that I wanted to see her, and besides, she wouldn't take long.*

*I replied again that I would not be able to see her and that she should make an appointment. Nevertheless, at lunchtime on Monday she came past the large sign that says the unit is closed between 12.30 and 1.30pm, and burst into my office, waving the cards that she said 'had sort of worked and sort of hadn't' in her exam – the week prior.*

Rachel is not registered with Disability Services and if she does identify as being on the spectrum, she has not mentioned it. She clearly has problems with executive function, professional communication, self-management, time management and applying the information she has learned. She was unable to register that the idea behind reporting back to me on how the study strategies were working for her was something that needed to be done during the study period, not after its completion when adjustments to it would be unhelpful. When I reported back to her referring body (in this case, a quite senior academic within the faculty), the academic volunteered that she also thought that perhaps Rachel was on the spectrum.

### Rachel

*Given that the remaining three subjects with which Rachel was struggling were the difference between her graduating at the end of the semester or being excluded from the university at the end of the semester, and given that she was convinced that her problem was purely about Mathematics, I arranged a joint consultation for her with a numeracy-focused Learning Development Lecturer. She agreed to this enthusiastically.*

*Rachel did not turn up to her appointment, and when reminded via email of the arrangement, replied blithely that she had forgotten, but that she would 'just look up her old Maths textbook' instead.*

*The next we heard from Rachel was when she copied Learning Development staff in to a response she sent to the administration of the university after being excluded from her course. In the email, Rachel included scanned copies of exam papers she had passed in earlier years, as proof that she was capable of 'passing an exam', and a detailed explanation of her ideas about how tutors could set her additional quizzes over the summer, how they could be adapted to allow her to look up information that suited her better, and how they could be graded. These allowances should be made, she argued, since she had 'sat in that class and taken notes for three years' and so didn't want to do it again. The fact that she had failed to prove that she had met the course requirements, or the requirements for graduation, eluded her.*

Rachel's rigid thinking led her to believe that she had a problem in Maths, so looking at a Maths textbook would help her. She failed to notice that she was having problems processing and applying the formulae – despite her own description of the exam problems that indicated this – believing that if she just learned the formulae she would be alright. She was unaware that an expert teacher in numeracy and Mathematics may be able to help her, that to suggest that such an expert could be easily replaced by reading a book might be insulting to that teacher, or that she had been employing that strategy and it had not worked. Further, when the strategy continued to be inadequate and she failed the subjects, leading to her exclusion from the course, she offered solutions that would limit the inconvenience to herself – with apparently no cognisance that the university had policies and procedures in place, that setting and marking extra work requires paying staff to do so, that the institution might consider it to be inequitable to effectively create an extra subject for the benefit of one student (let alone one who had not availed herself of the academic support that was offered) or that the ability to pass examinations in one context is not considered to be an adequate reason for a student not understanding later course material to be allowed to graduate.

## Conclusion

There is a positive side to the kind of pedantry and rigid thinking that we have described in this chapter: that a foregrounding of the mechanics of writing can be employed as a useful strategy once the requirements of the assignment are understood. Students will willingly replicate successful strategies about sentence and paragraph construction across a variety of contexts and assessments. Once they learn the expected requirement of assignment genres, students on the spectrum are typically able to reproduce it on demand.

Happily, many of our students on the spectrum do, after a false start or two, come to understand that their teachers have critical insider knowledge, and will defer to that knowledge. Others may take longer, and some may not complete their degrees on their first attempt as a result. This is to be expected with a spectrum disorder. As tertiary teachers, we can take responsibility for making teaching experiences, assessment tasks and expectations as explicit as possible in order to facilitate more of our students on the spectrum being part of that first graduating cohort.

## Tips for Teachers

- Adding in metaphors to explain something may actually not be helping all of your students. Try asking if another student can explain it, instead. Also ask your student with Autism Spectrum Disorder to explain what she or he understands (so far).

- Use synonyms and interchangeable or expanded forms of terms when referring to subject matter so that students are exposed to a range of appropriate vocabulary.

- Be patient. Explain more than you think you have to, especially for first-year students.

- Find time to discuss your expectations around classroom behaviour and assessment. If there isn't time to discuss in class, consider emailing or posting to the subject website or discussion site.

- Be prepared to explain the key features of assessment types ... or direct students to someone who can. We have included a list of common genre types in this chapter, but be careful to be explicit with your students (for example, say 'essay' or 'report' rather than 'assignment').

- Know the differences between reproductive, analytical and speculative learning, and explain them to your students, using appropriate examples drawn from your subject area. If interested in this area of theory, perhaps read the contributions of Ballard and Clanchy to the field of tertiary learning.

- Understand the 'Conditions for Learning' outlined in this chapter and *authentically* engage with your students.

- Use written instructions to reinforce oral ones – as you speak, write on the board.

- As you write on the board, create a word list of new vocabulary and ask students to consider copying it down.

- As you write on the board, construct a concept map related to what is being discussed.

## Tips for Learners

- Your way of thinking may be different from that of other people in the class. Try to view this as an opportunity for sharing their ideas and really listen to them. They may return the favour, and, remember, different viewpoints can lead to learning.

- Do not tell someone else that their idea is wrong. Learn some phrases to politely disagree, for example, 'I look at it a bit differently' or 'I didn't see it that way'.

- Even if you think a particular assignment or activity is silly, do not tell the lecturer, tutor or marker. You may be right, but the assessment is unlikely to change. Find ways to approach it that work for you.

- Read this chapter to better understand what is meant by particular assessment genre, such as essays, reports and several other things.

- You may well hate groupwork; many people do. Think about how you can make this less stressful for yourself. If you find that groups tend to waste time or waffle, you may need to take the lead, even if this is uncomfortable. Before meeting, think about which tasks you are happy or better able to do. Set an agenda. Taking a lead role may end up being easier than being saddled with tasks that no one else wants to do or that really don't suit your personality or learning style!

- Rigid thinking can extend to perfectionism. You do not have to work on something over and over until it is perfect. Sometimes, you have a lot of assignments due and worrying that something is not the best you could do is not helpful. It is OK to hand in an assignment if you genuinely think, 'This is the best I can do *right now.*'

- For some people on the spectrum, it can be hard to let the conversation in a tutorial or lecture move on. If you had a great idea you wanted to share but the conversation went somewhere else, coming back to that point may actually disrupt the flow of the conversation in the classroom. Sometimes you just have to let it go and move on. These days, many subjects have online discussion boards where you might be able to edit and post these thoughts if you still think that they are interesting or relevant to the topic being studied.

- Be aware that you may find dealing with the social aspects of the classroom very tiring. Have strategies and social stories prepared. See our 'Tips for Learners' in Chapter 3 for help with participation in classes, including lectures and tutorials.

# Chapter 5

# Project Planning and Multi-Tasking

Executive function and the ability to multi-task can be problematic areas for students on the spectrum. Executive dysfunction can manifest around task shifting, and working memory can have significant negative impacts on academic performance (Lijfft, Kenemans, Verbaten and van Engeland, 2005; Gawrilow, Gollwitzer and Oettingen, 2011), since it leads to problems with remembering and completing sub-tasks independently. It also leads to issues around inhibition (or a lack thereof), which may lead to the kinds of inappropriate behaviour we discussed in Chapter 3. Wolf and her colleagues summarise executive function problems thus: that students on the spectrum struggle to convert syllabus documents into a 'game plan... Many cannot surmount the demands of an academic calendar that insists they be able to multi-task, study for several exams at once, or have several long-range projects on the table at the same time' (Wolf, Thierfeld Brown and Kukiela Bork, 2009, p. 92). An impairment in executive function can impact on cognitive flexibility, behavioural adaptation to the environment, sorting essential from non-essential information, understanding codes of conduct and setting a goal and being able to work towards it (Freedman, 2010). Because students on the spectrum often find solace in routine, there is potential for them to establish routines that they hope will assist with the college or university workload, and not be able to recognise if they have become counterproductive, let alone adjust them. Once again, it becomes a matter of identifying the area of difficulty, suggesting useful strategies, and then guiding the students to internalise them.

A lesser-known but significant difference between Versions 4 and 5 of the *Diagnostic and Statistical Manual of Mental Disorders* was its overturning of the prohibition of diagnosing Attention Deficit Hyperactivity Disorder (ADHD) in the context of a Pervasive Developmental Disorder such as Autism Spectrum Disorder (American Psychiatric Association, 2013). The change allows for a more accurate collation of data about the high rates of comorbidity between Autism Spectrum Disorder and Attention Deficit Hyperactivity Disorder. Indeed, there is some scientific evidence to suggest that the two disorders originate from similar genetic factors (Antshel, Zhang-James and Faraone, 2013).

With assistance, students can develop strategies and rules to help manage the tertiary study workload, which inevitably involves competing deadlines. The transition to university or college can be confusing for any student. As John Harpur, Maria Lawlor and Michael Fitzgerald note, new students are 'explorer[s] in largely unfamiliar territory' (Harpur, Lawlor and Fitzgerald, 2004, p. 13). Semesters or trimesters mean that workloads are compressed and that while face-to-face contact hours may seem manageable, assessment seems to fit into a few short 'seasons' where students may have competing assignment or test work in all of their subjects simultaneously. For a compartmentalised thinker, this can be extremely challenging. Students who prefer to complete one task before beginning the next will almost inevitably become distressed when faced with competing deadlines of equal import – or, as is also possible, tasks due at around the same time but of significantly different value (such as an assignment worth 10 per cent of the subject being due one day, and one worth 40 per cent in a different subject being due the following day). Further, a reliance on learned 'rules' – for example, that one should try one's best in assessment tasks – may make it difficult for a student on the spectrum to take a pragmatic approach and recognise that under such circumstances, it is possible that they will not be able to complete all the work to their preferred standards if they are to meet all the deadlines.

## Blaine

*Blaine left school with inadequate grades for university entrance. He went to a foundation college before transferring into his local regional university.*

*At school, he had had a dedicated teacher's aide and in the college he was used to small numbers and literacy-based assessments. In his first semester at university he was faced with large lecture halls. He took a full load of four subjects; a foreign language, Philosophy, Psychology and an English Literature subject. Each of these disciplines at his institution used a different referencing system and set different styles of assessment tasks. The compressed nature of a 13-week teaching session means that assessment tasks are almost inevitably scheduled so that assessable work across multiple subjects falls due at the same time. In approximately Weeks 4, 9 and 13 of the semester, therefore, he was trying to juggle three or four assessment tasks, all with different parameters and expectations.*

*Blaine sought assistance from the Disabilities Liaison Office and Learning Development. He was assigned a Learning Development Lecturer who had a learning and teaching background in English literature and foreign languages. He sought assistance with time and life management, as well as with his written work. This was critical because Blaine did not always understand some social situations or expectations around working hours. For example, his appointments with the Learning Development Lecturers were on Wednesdays. When a public holiday fell on a Wednesday, he began trying to rearrange his social engagements for that day so that he could still come to Learning Development as usual – with no awareness that a public holiday is not just for students, but that the university itself would not be open, nor the staff member available.*

*Blaine did not always share the full story with regard to his studies. At various points he assured the Learning Development Lecturer that all was going well, only for her to be informed by the Disabilities Liaison Officer and/or the faculty teaching staff that the assessment had not been completed or had been submitted but was not worthy of a passing grade.*

Of course, the most simple way to ease students into the idea of competing deadlines is to minimise the number of them, at least initially. Indeed, it is often recommended that students on the spectrum consider taking fewer than the maximum number of course units in the early stages, to allow time to adjust to the new environment and academic requirements (Attwood, 2007; Bradshaw, 2013). This has been a strategy we have also often recommended to students, but we are also mindful that a reduced subject load can have financial implications for students who are in receipt of government funding to support their studies.

Executive function is basically the ability to develop a system of organisation. It refers to the set of skills employed in planning, foresight, and synthesising information (Wolf, Thierfeld Brown and Kukiela Bork, 2009). It stands to reason that executive *dysfunction* can be understood as a 'faulty internal organi[s]ational system' (Wolf, Thierfeld Brown and Kukiela Bork, 2009, p. 230), which impacts on the person's ability to plan, sequence, initiate and sustain behaviour toward goal achievement, or to make and incorporate adjustments as required. Poor executive function also impacts on working memory, impulse control, and understanding abstract concepts (Attwood, 2007), all of which are areas that we typically consider to be prerequisites for sustained success in a tertiary institution. Students on the spectrum commonly demonstrate some deficits in executive function, likely because they are often rigid, compartmentalised thinkers, who are not very good at the kind of internalisation or 'self-talk' that neurotypical people do in order to work out priorities. As we saw in the case study of James (Chapter 3), poor impulse or inhibitory control – the ability to restrain or inhibit responses and to self-regulate in certain situations – led to his use of inappropriate sexual innuendo with an academic member of staff. This inability to self-regulate in a formal teaching/learning situation demonstrated poor executive function. So students on the spectrum may need to be taught strategies to compensate for deficits in, and ultimately build, executive function.

## Strategies

Given that many students struggle to manage their time and the demands of competing deadlines, it is unrealistic to assume that our students on the spectrum will figure it out for themselves. They – alongside some of their neurotypical first-year peers – may need to have their attention drawn to the difference between contact hours or face-to-face teaching, and the amount of time that is expected to be dedicated to the subject. As an academic, you may need to check in with this cohort and ask some questions to find out whether they have some kind of plan in place. Do not just ask how everything is going, or if they have everything under control; they will be inclined to say yes! Students who have been successfully completing readings and turning up to class may feel as though they have a system working. That does not necessarily mean that they have factored in the time it takes to research, develop and edit an assignment, let alone more than one with due dates in close proximity to each other. Ask deeper questions – do you have a study timetable? What does it look like? When will you start working on your assignment? When do you think will you start writing? In our experience, these sorts of questions will alert you, as someone with experience in the university or college sector, to potential hurdles or roadblocks.

Tony Attwood argues that individuals on the spectrum typically have a predominantly visual style of thinking, and Thomas Armstrong posits that those on the spectrum are particularly good at systemisation (Armstrong, 2010; Attwood, 2007). When encouraging students to develop strategies for managing time and workload, therefore, it makes sense to encourage systems that rely on visual reminders – wall calendars, diaries, whiteboards, coloured highlighters and/or sticky notes, and so on (Wolf, Thierfeld Brown and Kukiela Bork, 2009).

The key to effective time management is task analysis. For most effective students, this means looking at when assessment items for each subject are due, and then collating these into one document or adding them to one calendar. Indeed, universities often provide students with a year planner, or they are available at newsagents and stationery stores at a reasonable price. Students on the spectrum, however, tend to be more compartmentalised thinkers and may dutifully arrange folders for each subject, without ever creating a master document that brings together assessment information for the entire semester. In order to build executive function, these students will need to create systems of organisation. They may need assistance with this process.

Once students have a sense of what is required overall, it is helpful to break each assessment task into smaller pieces. For example, a task analysis for an essay might read:

1. Review and understand question.

2. Figure out how you want to answer the question – the argument, broadly speaking, that will be used.

3. Research the question to provide evidence for this stance.

4. Plan the components of your essay.

5. Write the essay.

6. Edit and proofread the essay.

7. Check the bibliography and submit.

When students undertake this sort of task analysis, they typically become less inclined to attempt to write the essay the night before it is due.

For the many students on the spectrum who are perfectionists (Attwood, 2007), like Blaine or Esther (whom we met in Chapter 2), this can also help combat procrastination or over-focusing on one sub-task. Often even very capable students will find that they err on the side of over-researching: the process of reading someone else's thoughts tends to feel much safer than committing one's own thoughts to paper. Setting mini-deadlines for the sub-tasks may help.

### Blaine

*I asked Blaine to 'map' his remaining assessment tasks on the university-provided student wall planner. We wrote these in pen, and highlighted them. Thus he could easily see which weeks contained assessment tasks with competing deadlines.*

*We then brainstormed the sub-tasks for each assignment. Blaine was asked to estimate how long he might need on each sub-task. We then wrote these, in pencil, as mini-deadlines. Blaine could now see the point at which he needed to stop reading (looking for an elusive, perfect insight) and start writing (in order to submit the essay and have the opportunity to earn marks).*

Be aware that some students on the spectrum may not have great insight into how long things take, especially in their first year. You may need to gently suggest adjustments to the plan if it is clearly unrealistic.

### Paul

*Paul had numerous assignments due, all now under extensions. With three weeks of the semester left, he had more than 60 per cent of the assessment still to be completed in one subject, and 100 per cent of another. I asked Paul how many hours each part of his assignments was likely to take. Paul appeared to be wildly underestimating the complexity of the tasks at hand. At the end, I added up his time estimates for all the sub-tasks, and asked, 'So, you're saying it will only take about four hours to complete this entire assignment?' Paul looked most offended: 'Oh, I shouldn't think so,' he said, as though the idea had been mine, 'it would take much longer than that!'*

Breaking each assignment into a plan may also help students to resist diverging onto a tangent that is of interest but does not really address the assigned question (Wolf, Thierfeld Brown and Kukiela Bork, 2009). In other cases, we have seen students who engaged with the topic and the concerns of the assignment well, but were unable to restrict a topic they found interesting to the assigned word limit.

### Frank

*Frank was a bright but largely uncommunicative student who I suspected may be on the spectrum. When the first assignment neared, Frank stayed behind in my tutorial class and asked a question about word limits. I gave the standard response that the word limit was a good guide and included a tolerance of about 10 per cent either way, but added that I didn't mind if the student 'went over that a little bit' as long as the assignment was well written and on topic. 'Oh, good,' replied Frank, and with a flick of the wrist he unfurled a home-made scroll of pages taped together that went the length of the classroom. Essentially, he had written an Honours thesis on the book in question, when what was required was a 1500-word, first-year essay. I agreed to mark it and found that it was on topic, well written and well constructed; worthy of the highest possible grade. Most tutors, of course, would have stopped reading when they met the accepted word limit, and that was a lesson that Frank did need to learn, but he was not forced into doing so at that point in time!*

Examinations and tests provide another set of potential hurdles. Students with poor executive function may also have poor working memory; that is, the capacity to keep information in the forefront of their minds while thinking about how to apply that information in a problem-solving capacity. Further, the internal memory retrieval systems may not be as swift for a learner with Autism Spectrum Disorder as for his or her neurotypical peers. Students who are nervous, anxious, or worried about adhering to social codes in an exam room – which is, after all, a highly artificial and rule-bound environment – effectively have less cognitive ability left over to deal with the task at hand. It is for this reason that an increasing proportion of students on the spectrum are being offered reasonable adjustments in the form of extra time, small group or solo examination provisions.

Students on the spectrum should, in the first instance, be offered the exam advice that works for *all* students: start preparations early, select relevant material, be aware of the exam format and revise accordingly, seek explanations if there are things that are not making sense, hone memory techniques, calculate – and stick to – the marks per minute, and use calming or relaxation techniques if it begins to feel insurmountable. Students on the spectrum, however, may require further guidance in exam preparation and techniques. As much as we might assert that university or college is not like school and that adult learners need to move away from being 'spoon fed', we also need to recognise that this cohort is not one that intuitively understands contextual changes. Therefore, we do have an additional duty of care to provide them with more explicit instructions and support until they are able to generalise and maintain academic expectations. Students may need assistance in developing study planners or timetables, and to be reminded that the number of hours required will need to be increased when exams or tests are imminent, even if they have established good routines for understanding new work throughout the semester. Retrieving older information is a different process and therefore will require more time and focus, and may require different strategies, such as constructing study notes. It is important that students understand early what many of their peers discover by trial and error: that cramming does not work; that hours and hours of study without a break is not effective, and that study sessions should be task-focused. Further, a surprising number of students need to be taught how to study, and that it is a different process from *re-reading*. It may be a good idea to model note-taking methods such as the Cornell method (which involves placing margins on either side of the note-taking space; the column on the left is used to label the notes in the middle; and the far right column is used to annotate links or connections to other materials, or make notes about initial responses or things that may need further explanation) or concept-mapping (sometimes known as mind-mapping).

| Bibliographic or lecture information | | |
|---|---|---|
| Keyword/ label | | Annotations/ links |
| | | |
| | | |
| | | |
| | | |

Figure 5.1: Cornell note-taking

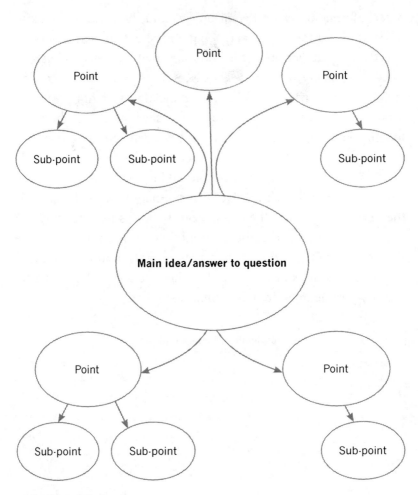

**Figure 5.2: Mind map**

Many students on the spectrum are highly visual learners, for whom a mind map will work well. Still others find them to be chaotic and overwhelming. Generally speaking, mind maps are a good way to place thoughts on a topic in one place. For many of us, however, they are not the most efficient way of organising those thoughts. A strategy we recommend is using the mind map to then create a much more linear plan.

| |
|---|
| Introduction |
| Paragraph 1 – idea: |
| Paragraph 2 – idea: |
| Paragraph 3 – idea: |
| Paragraph 4 – idea: |
| Paragraph 5 – idea: |
| Conclusion |

**Figure 5.3: Linear 'translation' of mind map**

Finally, the concept of practising timed responses is not one that occurs naturally to many students, let alone those who may have problems around executive function. Students may also need to be explicitly told to turn off distractions (such as phones or televisions) in order to better emulate exam conditions and therefore understand how much they can produce in the allocated time period. This will allow the student to make better choices about which ideas to include under exam conditions.

The student on the spectrum has additional needs. Organising and planning essays can be problematic at the best of times, let alone under exam conditions. Following instructions is another area that can require extra time and focus (Wolf, Thierfeld Brown and Kukiela Bork, 2009); things that are in short supply under exam conditions. Students on the spectrum may also have problems with processing speed, managing distraction and sensory issues within the exam room. We therefore need to make sure that the element of surprise is reduced and that students are going to enter the room feeling relatively prepared. Classroom teachers may do this by asking questions of the student to check for understanding; academics and others who offer support on a withdrawal basis may have the opportunity to take more time explaining the requirements and teaching compensatory strategies. We are all relatively well-positioned to notice if the student appears to be displaying maladaptive behaviours, and to encourage them to have plans in place in case there are unexpected glitches within the student's study timetable. It is important to explain to these students that plans require some degree of flexibility. In the same way that we would not progress with a planned tutorial if it became apparent that students in our classes had numerous questions about an upcoming assessment task, so too can we encourage our students on the spectrum to view a plan as a living document that can be slightly altered if necessary. While this does create a little more work for teaching academics, it arguably creates less work than, for example, a student having a public meltdown because a train strike meant that they could not get to the library on time to begin their scheduled block of study.

Invigilators may also need to be aware of the students' particular needs. Autism Spectrum Disorder is highly comorbid with anxiety issues. For many students, reading and re-reading the exam questions and writing some points may help to formulate a response. In some examinations, 'jotting down' points during the time allocated for reading is not permitted, and students will need to be alerted to this fact. If they need to be permitted to make notes during the reading period, then arrangements will need to be made in advance for a small group or solo examination to take place at the same time as the exam for the main group. For students with anxiety, re-reading the question or attempting to brainstorm some ideas may only serve to confirm that they do not understand the question (Bradshaw, 2013). Panic can lead to inappropriate exam room behaviours, and in some cases, such disturbances can have both academic and disciplinary consequences. This is another reason why small group or solo examination practices may be recommended for students on the spectrum.

## Assignments

Even though the assessment 'seasons' are predictable to experienced university staff and students, it can come as an enormous shock to newly enrolled students. The first week or even two weeks of the semester often seem to contain a lot of 'housekeeping' information and, indeed, tutorials may not start until the second week, lulling students into a false sense of security around the commitment associated with their studies. A couple of weeks later, however, the first assessment task is often a 'wake-up call', with students finding that they may not have left enough time to adequately prepare, write, reference and edit. For those students on the spectrum who are very task-oriented and like to focus on a single task until its completion, this can be a particularly difficult time. One assignment may be done to a standard bordering on perfection, for example, while another two are haphazardly thrown together close to the deadline, because the student felt unable to move on to another task until the first was completed.

For these students, creating sub-tasks is crucial. As Wolf *et al.* note, many beginning students may have become used to parents and aides assisting them to break down their assignments for them (Wolf, Thierfeld Brown and Kukiela Bork, 2009). Subject outlines may give the students some preliminary ideas about what needs to be done, but many will still need a staged or scaffolded approach in order to develop and internalise the assessment literacies required.

We begin by offering students the kinds of tangible supports that assist executive function: student diaries, wall planners, weekly planners and so on. The suite of tools used will obviously be tailored according to how the student works best, but in almost all cases a wall planner is a crucial visual reminder. It shows students at a glance when assessment-heavy times are coming up (unlike a diary, where turning the page and finding that two assignments are due Monday is an unmitigated disaster – diaries should only be used in tandem with a bigger picture plan).

In the digital age, it is easy for students to supplement the larger visual plan with portable weekly calendars and so on, so that they can 'budget' their time. In addition to basic calendars and reminders, there are numerous organisational applications that students can use, that will sync with their phones and other devices. Software and mobile applications or 'apps' such as *Wunderlist* allow students to set reminders about required readings, assignments and exams, with functions to organise repeat or one-off deadlines, a 'starring' system to help with prioritisation, and the ability to view commitments either according to theme or the closeness of the deadline. Audible reminders are sent when tasks are not completed by the date entered into the app.

Budgeting or planning time may require explicit conversations around marking weightings and so on. If a student has three assignments due in one week, the first instinct may be to prioritise according to deadline. If all assignments were of equal weighting, this would work well. If, however, the first assignment is worth 5 per cent and the third one worth 50 per cent, then clearly it makes more sense to allocate time according to the weighting; something that may not be immediately apparent to the student. For example, in the current first-year Primary Education programme at our institution, in the first semester students can expect the following assessment schedule in Weeks 4 through 6:

**Week 4:** 1000-word essay; 15-minute numeracy quiz; language and literacy tutorial task

**Week 5:** number mastery exam, 15-minute quiz; tutorial task

**Week 6:** two-hour mid-session exam; 15-minute quiz; write and submit a lesson plan + 500-word reflection.

**Table 5.1: Allocating time to the assessment schedule according to assessment weightings**

| | | Weighting | Week |
|---|---|---|---|
| **1000-word essay** | • Figure out what the question is asking. Do I need to double-check with teaching staff and/or Learning Development to check I'm on the right track?<br>• Break the question into parts and look at the word limit. How many words on each section, approximately?<br>• Preliminary research<br>• Plan essay<br>• Write<br>• Redraft<br>• Get a 'critical friend' or Learning Development Lecturer to offer feedback<br>• Implement suggested changes<br>• Final editing<br>• Referencing<br>• Check the submission requirements (how to submit; what formatting is required; what time is the actual deadline) | 20% | 4 |
| **15-minute numeracy quiz** | • Check the scope of the quiz<br>• Gather notes from those weeks' lectures and tutorials<br>• Revision time<br>• Practice questions time | 5% | 4 |
| **Language and literacy tutorial task** | • Check what is required<br>• Allocate time to write<br>• Allocate time to edit | 15% | 4 |

*cont.*

| | | Weighting | Week |
|---|---|---|---|
| **Number mastery exam** | • Check the scope of the exam<br>• Gather notes from those weeks' lectures and tutorials<br>• Revision time<br>• Practice questions time | 15% | 5 |
| **15-minute quiz** | • Check the scope of the quiz<br>• Gather notes from those weeks' lectures and tutorials<br>• Revision time<br>• Practice questions time | 15% | 5 |
| **Tutorial task** | • Check what is required<br>• Allocate time to write<br>• Allocate time to edit | 20% | 5 |
| **Two-hour mid-session exam** | • Check the scope of the exam<br>• Gather notes from those weeks' lectures and tutorials<br>• Revision time<br>• Practice questions time | 40% | 6 |
| **15-minute quiz** | • Gather notes from those weeks' lectures and tutorials<br>• Revision time<br>• Practice questions time | 5% | 6 |
| **Write and submit a lesson plan + 500-word reflection** | • Decide the focus/scope/sequence of the lesson<br>• State how that fits with the syllabus<br>• State how/why it is suitable for this class at this time<br>• Make a note of the resources you need<br>• Think about a mix of different kinds of learning and teaching activities and how long you need on each<br>• Leave time to write reflection<br>• You may need to do some brief research on how to be a 'reflective practitioner' as this is not something that is often covered in secondary school | 25% | 6 |

A student who wants to complete the task on which she or he is focusing before moving on to the next one is likely to run into problems in the first of these weeks; if the essay 'needs' to be completed before any study can happen it is unlikely that the student will pass the quiz; and if the student is cramming for the quiz before their tutorial in one subject, it is possible that they will not have time to adequately prepare for the tutorial task in another subject. Of the three tasks due in Week 4, the final one on the list, the tutorial task (15 per cent), is worth more than the middle task (the 5 per cent quiz), so it should ideally be started earlier and be given about three times as much time as studying for the quiz, since it is worth three times as many marks. Similarly, two of the tasks in Week 6 – the mid-session and the lesson plan activity – are likely to require significant time allocation and therefore may need to be started in Week 5, even though there are other (but smaller) assessment tasks in that week.

A more sensible approach than a purely chronological one, then, is to break the tasks into sub-tasks. For example, the student needs to understand the components of each task. Students on the spectrum may well need this kind of hidden curriculum to be explicated for them. Rather than a series of nine tasks on a wall calendar, then, the following 'to do' list-approach may be useful:

- prep for essay

- write essay

- check/proofread/edit essay

- study for quiz

- prep for tutorial task

- write tutorial task

- check/proofread/edit tutorial task

- study for exam

- study for quiz 2

- prep for tutorial task 2

- write tutorial task 2

- check/proofread/edit tutorial task 2

- study for quiz 3

- write lesson plan

- reflect on lesson plan.

The length of this list should help you to convince the student that they will not be able to do things 'the night before' and maintain their sanity or health, let alone any kind of educational standard. Some students will need significant assistance to approximate how long each of the sub-tasks might be expected to take and figure out how to write a study timetable in such a way as to make the whole process manageable. It is a good idea to check the schedule/outline proposed by the student, and make sure that it is a plan that will assist success, rather than a document doomed to failure.

Next, help the student to identify which are the 'bigger'/more time-consuming tasks, by looking at the sub-task lists. If there is more to do in order to meet assignment requirements, more time should be allocated. Conversely, there may be some areas where a 'well-used 15 minutes' (Martin, 2011, p. 41) can be strategically employed. If there are some sub-tasks that utilise lower-order thinking skills (such as retaining and reproducing knowledge without application), flashcards – either physical or digital, again using mobile apps – can be constructed and reviewed while using public transport or other similar times that might otherwise have been used unproductively. Many students struggle to budget their time, and those on the spectrum may have associated executive function problems, so establishing time-management strategies is best done, at least in the first instance, as a guided activity. Using a proforma such as the one in Figure 5.4, encourage students to mark in pen those activities that are the same every week, and non-negotiable (such as tutorial and lecture attendance). Then, encourage them to photocopy enough 'weeks' to represent the weeks left in the semester (most study planners fail because students try to make every week look the same, and this is rarely the case – especially when assessments are due).

PLANNER FOR THE WEEK OF: [                    ]     WEEKLY GOALS: [                    ]

| DATE: | Monday | Tuesday | Wednesday | Thursday | Friday | Saturday | Sunday |
|---|---|---|---|---|---|---|---|
| 8:00 AM | | | | | | | |
| 8:30 AM | | | | | | | |
| 9:00 AM | | | | | | | |
| 9:30 AM | | | | | | | |
| 10:00 AM | | | | | | | |
| 10:30 AM | | | | | | | |
| 11:00 AM | | | | | | | |
| 11:30 AM | | | | | | | |
| 12:00 PM | | | | | | | |
| 12:30 PM | | | | | | | |
| 1:00 PM | | | | | | | |
| 1:30 PM | | | | | | | |
| 2:30 PM | | | | | | | |
| 3:00 PM | | | | | | | |
| 3:30 PM | | | | | | | |
| 4:00 PM | | | | | | | |
| 4:30 PM | | | | | | | |
| 5:00 PM | | | | | | | |
| 5:30 PM | | | | | | | |
| 6:00 PM | | | | | | | |
| 6:30 PM | | | | | | | |
| 7:00 PM | | | | | | | |
| 7:30 PM | | | | | | | |
| 8:00 PM | | | | | | | |
| 8:30 PM | | | | | | | |

**Figure 5.4: Time planner**

Now encourage the students to write in other commitments, such as meetings with support staff one a month, a meeting with group members to complete an assessment, or work shifts. Students should be encouraged to have the timetable reflect reality, not to become a modern-day instrument of torture – there is no point deciding to study while *Doctor Who* is on if you are only going to sit there resenting the fact that you are not watching *Doctor Who*, and no point 'planning' to study for six hours on the same Saturday if it is Grandma's birthday and all the cousins are coming for a rare visit (unless the student is planning to use studying as a means of retiring from social interaction). Once these commitments are marked in, the remaining blocks of time are the ones that are available for study and assignments. Generally, students should pencil in a plan that enables them to cycle through their subjects, but when a particular task is due, it will take priority. If students find that they are unable to concentrate on a particular task at that time, encourage them to swap it with another task elsewhere on the plan (hence the pencil!). Ask students to identify which times of day are most productive for them, and encourage them to do the subjects with which they have the most difficulty at the times when they are most alert. The more difficult or boring work may need to be broken into sections (Martin, 2011). Any less-cognitive tasks (such as reading a set text, reviewing lecture notes, or listening once more to a recorded lecture) can be scheduled for times when the student is less likely to have the intense clarity of thought required for more demanding tasks, such as writing essays.

Finally, make sure students check the weighting column. One of the authors has very clear memories of spending hours collating and commenting on newspaper articles for a first-year subject. While she was rewarded with a High Distinction and high praise from the lecturer, a more pragmatic college mate pointed out that it was only a 5 per cent assignment and thus all of those hours had resulted in only 4.75 marks. In the instance above, it would be a mistake to hastily cobble together the Week 6 lesson plan and reflection merely because they are last on the list, given that they are worth 25 per cent of the marks in that subject.

We can reasonably expect that some students will find it difficult to change their thinking with regard to juggling sub-tasks across multiple subjects and assignments. Some will stubbornly insist on doing the assignment that is due first, first, and so on.

### Blaine

*Blaine would write and rewrite the introduction to his assignments, seeking perfection, and never move onto the next task, no matter what schedule had been devised. At one point he admitted that he was only sleeping between two and four hours a night. When things became particularly overwhelming, he gave himself a 'time out' where he left his desk and sat outside by himself for half an hour as a circuit breaker. While this strategy was to be applauded, it did little to ease his overall anxiety as when he returned to his studies he felt 'even further behind'.*

In this kind of situation, it can be helpful to add external accountability. 'Check-In Check-Out' (CICO) is a typically school-based intervention for students with additional behavioural needs (Campbell and Anderson, 2011). It provides students with instruction about desired behaviour, increases structured contacts between teachers and students, provides a mechanism for formal feedback on behaviour, and increases opportunities for reinforcement of expected behaviour (Campbell and Anderson, 2011). The components typically include morning and afternoon meetings with a nominated intervention co-ordinator, scheduled monitoring and feedback from teachers, a token economy (where students earn tokens and rewards as positive reinforcement for desired behaviours and habits) and contact with home (Campbell and Anderson, 2011; Hawken and Horner, 2003). There is significant evidence to suggest that it reduces the frequency of problem behaviour and increases academic engagement (Hawken and Horner, 2003; March and Horner, 2002). A modified form of CICO can be useful for university students. A virtual check-in/check-out ensures that the student remains in contact, and email conversations provide feedback, a small measure of external accountability, and redirection to next steps, if required. This simple strategy can provide a new 'rule' and go some way to counteracting any perfectionist tendencies.

### Blaine

*Blaine was required to email every week and update on how reality and his work plan were coalescing. This provided an external 'check' that went some way to counteract the obsessive or perfectionist thoughts to which he could be prone. Although this did not solve all of his problems, the percentage of times when he submitted assessment tasks on time did improve.*

### Esther

*Esther used 'Check-In Check-Out' to assist her in a weight loss programme. Over a six-month period she sent a daily email to her weight loss coach outlining what she planned to eat the following day. Because of her 'rule-following' nature, she stuck to what she planned and lost 30 kilograms!*

'Check-In Check-Out' can also be a useful tool for overcoming writers' block. Conventional wisdom suggests that when writing is difficult, the best solution is to just write *something* – but it may be hard to convince a person on the spectrum who has significant time pressures that writing words that they may reject later is a good use of that limited time.

In Chapter 2, we discussed assessment literacies: understanding the implications of questions and the requirements of answers. While students are learning to comprehend these ideas and internalise strategies, they may take some missteps. A good working relationship with a Learning Development Lecturer or similar academic adviser can constitute an important safety net, in this instance. Having the ability to share a plan or draft with an academic who is independent of the faculty affords the student an opportunity to reassess and redirect their efforts if an answer appears to be heading off on a tangent.

It may be that the student does not wish to seek 'outside' help, but you have established a working relationship wherein they consult you for discipline-specific writing advice. If the student is on the right track, this can be quite a pleasant teaching interaction, as long as you keep in mind the ideas we are canvassing in this book: that you may need to make explicit expectations and codes of conduct; that you may need to adjust for potentially rigid or literal thinking; that students may struggle to independently project-plan or self-monitor; and that central coherence may still be developing. This is all made more difficult if the student has misinterpreted assignment expectations, and can be a tricky area to negotiate. First of all, there is always an art to gently telling a learner that they are wrong, particularly if they have already made a significant investment of study time. This is, of course, potentially more difficult if the student is a rigid thinker. It is not unheard of for us to have students tell us that the marker, or indeed, the question is wrong. There is a further implication in terms of the time budget, however; scarce study time resources need to be reallocated if the requirements of the assignments have not been met in the first attempt. Here it is a matter of calmly retracing the process, all the while being aware that the student is likely to be (quite rightly) agitated and upset that they have to 're-do' that which they felt was already done.

### *Blaine*

*Blaine was understandably anxious about 're-doing' assignment work within a reduced timeframe. A new list of tasks was drawn up and time allocated accordingly.*

*Although Blaine did make it through the semester with scraping passes, after extensive discussions with his Disability Liaison Officer, he ultimately decided that he was not really ready for university studies and would be better to work for a few years and return when he had a clear idea of which subjects he wanted to study. At that point, he reasoned, he would be able to refine the number of subjects he was studying and perhaps streamline the expectations and referencing systems to those specific to a single discipline.*

## Conclusion

Students may need to develop and use a series of supports in order to manage competing deadlines. Ultimately, of course, the aim is for the student to be able to apply these processes independently. Students on the spectrum are likely to require more support in learning to internalise strategies, and, even when strategies have been successful in one context or subject, may need to be reminded that they are transferable.

### Tips for Teachers

- If students seem stuck on a particular task or project (such as a group assignment), ask them if they have done anything like this before, and if any strategies worked particularly well. Sometimes they just need to be reminded to transfer a strategy from one context to another.

- Use visual reminders (for example, add a note to a slide, or have a class calendar on the subject website) to help students have an understanding of when tasks or assignments are due.

### Tips for Learners

- Get hold of a year planner and mark deadlines in pen and highlighter. Pencil in sub-deadlines to keep you on track. Place it where you can see it – and where the people with whom you live can see it, too, so that they can be supportive of your endeavours.

- Create a weekly time budget. This will (usually!) reassure you that you are going to be able to get everything done.

If your time budget suggests that perhaps you will not make all your deadlines, either revise it or contact appropriate staff to explain your situation and ask whether you might be eligible for an extension.

- Use visual reminders where possible – colour helps to remind you which idea belongs in which subject. Also consider buying folders for each subject and get in the habit of filing information according to subjects and topics, rather than leaving them all in the folder you carry with you to university or college.

- Break difficult or boring work into sections, rather than trying to 'power through'. Schedule breaks where you can get some sunshine, exercise, food, or just relax for a short while.

- Schedule your hardest tasks or subjects for when you are most alert. Have a list of 'low-impact' study tasks that you can revert to when you are feeling tired.

- Are there any small and portable learning tasks or activities required? Consider making flashcards or using flashcard applications on your phone so that you can study on the bus or train (as an added bonus, if you look busy, strangers are less likely to attempt to engage you in small talk!).

- If you are struggling with procrastination and/or perfectionism, see if you can find a trusted peer or staff member with whom you can regularly 'check in'. External accountability is a wonderful motivator.

# Chapter 6

# Self-Monitoring

As we have already noted, university and college students are expected to demonstrate a higher level of independence within their studies than their younger counterparts; managing their own workloads and deadlines and organising their own study materials (Palmer, 2006). We also recognise that for students with autism, who typically find it more difficult to decode these unwritten expectations and who may have problems with executive function, independence may be a goal that can only be achieved with scaffolded, effective, evidence-based interventions. While the strategies we have outlined in earlier chapters will assist to build the academic capacity of students on the spectrum, it is likely that some students may also require systems, strategies and interventions in order to maintain, generalise and internalise them.

Autism Spectrum Disorder is effectively a social disability that is predicated on a social processing disorder (Gaus, 2011). Those on the spectrum are often idiosyncratic in the ways that they process both social and non-social information (Gaus, 2011). Research indicates that individuals on the spectrum have some impaired metacognition; specifically, in the area of metamemory. Since metacognition, or 'thinking about thinking' (Grainger, Williams and Lind, 2014a) plays an important role in self-regulation and essentially requires 'mindreading' from those who may be 'mindblind', it is sometimes regarded as applied Theory of Mind (Flavell, 2000). Metamemory refers to the metacognitive processes of monitoring and control; the awareness and ability to regulate current mental activity and mental states (Grainger, Williams and Lind, 2014a). Impaired metamemory, therefore, leads to problems with time management and problem solving; two areas with which individuals on the spectrum often have difficulty (Hewitt, 2011; Strnadova and Cumming, 2016). It is considered essential for adaptive functioning, since it allows individuals to read responses to their own behaviour and tailor it accordingly (Grainger, Williams and Lind, 2014b), something that can be difficult for students on the spectrum, as we have seen in the various case studies, and that rather self-evidently has implications for educational practice. If, for example, a student cannot accurately assess which information they know well and which they need to strengthen, they will not be able to prioritise their study timetables accordingly (Grainger, Williams and Lind, 2014b). Similarly, the inability to accurately assess one's own progress within a subject or course leads to the procrastination-perfectionism loop that we have discussed previously. Students like Blaine and Esther find themselves unable to recognise either when they are on track for an excellent mark in a subject, or likely to fail spectacularly. Nor are they able to adjust the amount of time devoted to the subject accordingly, opting instead, in many cases, to work obsessively and unnecessarily for hours or even days on end; or conversely, to persist with a completely inadequate study regime without recognition that information is not being learned or retained.

Developing metacognitive skills will assist students in their classroom behaviour, time management and anxiety management and has even been found to 'remediate difficulties in reading, writing and mathematical reasoning' (Grainger, Williams and Lind, 2014a, p. 657). It is clearly very important, therefore, that students within an adult learning environment, such as a university or college, learn, generalise and maintain these skills. The key difficulty here is that while we, as teachers, can adapt our teaching practices in order to have a better chance of students understanding the material, and we can advise them on strategies to revise the material, self-monitoring is something over which we have far less influence, since it is ultimately incumbent upon the student to take responsibility for developing and using these skills. We can only alert them to what they might try, and allow them the opportunities to do so. It is important, however, to be supportive of such strategies when a student is attempting to engage with them, and this will require significant sensitivity on the part of the teacher. If you are in a lecture hall or tutorial classroom, for example, and a student seems to be checking her or his phone every five minutes, it is statistically more probable that the student concerned is a neurotypical one having a conversation via text message or social media platform, than a student on the spectrum checking her or his own focus or on-task behaviour. Nevertheless, your response is critical; if the latter proves to be the case and you have publicly commented negatively on the behaviour or directed the student to put the phone away, the student is unlikely to persist with the strategy, even if it was proving to be a useful one.

Self-monitoring has been described as a lifelong skill that is applicable in many facets of daily life (Williams and Happé, 2009); a 'covert process involving self-assessment and self-recording, enabling an individual to become more aware of whether he/she is performing a specific task' (Finn, Ramasay, Dukes and Scott, 2015, p. 1408). Self-monitoring, therefore, is a means of teaching students the skills critical to compensate for diminished executive function, and improving their time management, ability to acquire and comprehend new information, meet deadlines and perform multi-step processes (Finn, Ramasay, Dukes and Scott, 2015), but, more critically, to teach them how to be able to draw on those skills without prompting from a peer, mentor or teacher. It has long been established that individuals on the spectrum have diminished understanding of some of the psychological aspects of self (Grainger, Williams and Lind, 2014a; Hurlbert, Happé and Frith, 1994; Williams and Happé, 2010). It is also well established that people with the disorder have superior memory for actions they have performed themselves, rather than those they have observed (Baker-Ward, Hess and Flannagan, 1990; Engelkamp, 1998; Grainger, Williams and Lind, 2014a). It is unrealistic, therefore, to expect that as long as we offer students on the spectrum advice about how to go about their learning at university or college, they will be able to apply that advice across a range of different academic situations. It is more likely that it will take both time and overt commitment from the student for the strategies to be automated. It is also likely that support from you, as teachers, will better facilitate the internalisation of those strategies as the student moves from requiring the assistance of more capable others to having automatised and fossilised the learning (Gallimore and Tharp, 1990).

Self-monitoring is an ongoing process of students collecting and collating information about their own on- and off-task behaviours and their impact on academic language and learning (Stasolla, Perilli and Daniani, 2014). Ideally, it should involve proactive interventions that can be individualised and adapted to a range of settings (Finn, Ramasay, Dukes and Scott, 2015). A number of studies have shown that training in self-monitoring assists students to increase their attention, on-task behaviour, and academic productivity (Anderson and Wheldall, 2004; Callahan and Rademacher, 1999; Farrell and McDougall, 2008; Finn, Ramasay, Dukes and Scott, 2015; Holifield, Goodman, Hazelkorn and Heflin, 2010; Legge, DeBar and Alber-Morgan, 2010; Soares, Vannest and Harrison, 2009).

Self-monitoring consists of two stages: measurement and evaluation (Loftin, Gibb and Skiba, 2005). The student must first decide which behaviour is going to be measured, how it will be measured, and then commit to measuring it. In the second stage, this data is compared with a pre-determined standard (Wright, 2013). Self-monitoring may utilise low- or high-technology strategies, or a combination of both. It encourages the student to become a responsible participant in the intervention (Wright, 2013), which encourages the kind of independent learning that universities and colleges typically envisage among their graduate outcomes.

The steps involved in self-monitoring are: defining the target behaviours to self-monitor; choosing a method for recording the self-monitoring data; choosing a self-monitoring schedule; deciding on a monitoring cue; choosing rewards for successful behaviour change; conducting periodic accuracy checks; and fading the self-monitoring plan. For students on the Autism Spectrum who are already negotiating the new social environment of the university, as well as attempting to keep up with the learning tasks and assessments within the subjects in which they are enrolled, this list must seem unrealistically exhaustive. It is clear that students on the spectrum may need support in many, if not all, of these steps.

In the first step of defining a behaviour suitable for monitoring, it may be that the student needs assistance in understanding which behaviours need to be decreased, increased or adapted. Directions must be very clear; telling a student with a social disability to 'behave appropriately' is largely a pointless exercise. Instead, define clear markers against which the student can monitor her or his progress, such as 'I will stay in my seat for the entire tutorial' or 'I will raise my hand and quietly ask to be excused if I am feeling over-stimulated and want to leave', for example. The student must be able to easily identify whether or not the goal is being achieved, so the required behaviours must be clearly identified.

In terms of deciding how to record the data, there are three main options: a rating scale, a checklist or a frequency count (Wright, 2013). A rating or Likert scale asks students to qualitatively rate how well they did at meeting a goal. A checklist is more binary and requires fewer evaluative processes – students must only make a call as to whether they did or did not achieve the goal on the checklist. A frequency count requires students to keep a running tally of the times that a target behaviour is displayed (Wright, 2013). Timed cues are used as reminders to check for the target behaviour and make a mark in the tally column. It is the option most frequently used in schools, so some younger university or college students may find it to be a familiar process.

**Rating Scale**
How well did I...

1. Stay on task?

        Poor     Fair     Good     Excellent

2. Adhere to my study schedule?

        Poor     Fair     Good     Excellent

3. Remain seated in my tutorial this week?

        Poor     Fair     Good     Excellent

**Figure 6.1: Rating scale**

**Checklist**
Did I...

1. Stay on task?                                              YES/NO

2. Adhere to my study schedule?                  YES/NO

3. Remain seated in my tutorial this week?      YES/NO

**Figure 6.2: Checklist**

**Rating Scale**

I engaged in these behaviours:

1. Focusing on what the lecturer was saying as each slide was explained:

| Date | Tally | Total |
|------|-------|-------|
|      |       |       |
|      |       |       |

2. Making notes as I went through the prescribed readings:

| Date | Tally | Total |
|------|-------|-------|
|      |       |       |
|      |       |       |
|      |       |       |
|      |       |       |

**Figure 6.3: Frequency count**

The third step is choosing the self-monitoring schedule. With children and adolescents, this typically means deciding whether the behaviour will be monitored at the start of the day, at the end of the day, at scheduled transition points throughout the day, at fixed intervals throughout the day, or at the start or end of assignments (Wright, 2013). Within the tertiary education context, it is most likely that the most appropriate times for students to choose to monitor their behaviour will be within certain subjects or within certain class types (such as lectures or tutorials), as well as during assignment preparation and completion.

Step 4 is creating a monitoring cue, and is an area wherein the teacher may have a very clearly defined role. The teacher can deliver a cue (such as a relatively surreptitious hand gesture) to remind the student to self-monitor. Alternatively, students may self-administer a cue, such as a sound or, more likely in terms of not disrupting the lesson, a silent or vibrating alarm. This is more socially appropriate for adult learners in large classes, and in the discussion below we will examine some of the systems that students can utilise for this purpose.

The fifth step is optional and involves establishing rewards for successfully changing the behaviour. Ultimately the goal is always for the student to develop their social and academic skills to the point where they are intrinsically motivated to generalise and maintain appropriate behaviours. That said, the entire university sector is predicated on extrinsic rewards in the form of grades, and even adults can find external treats or rewards to be extremely motivating.

### Rosa

*Rosa enrolled in an Arts degree at university when she was in her early fifties. In addition to Autism Spectrum Disorder, she had complex mental and physical health issues. Rosa undertook a workload of only one subject per semester, and enlisted the support of Disabilities Liaison, Learning Development and Counselling to assist her in her studies.*

*Rosa did not have family or adult friends within the local area. She expressed on several occasions that she felt that she was missing out on opportunities to 'just talk about' the novels she was reading in the course of her studies. When Rosa was working on improving her time management and preparedness skills, I suggested that we could hold our appointments in the less formal environment of a campus coffee shop, instead of my office, in our own mini book club – during the weeks when she emailed me to confirm that she had read the novels and was prepared for her classes.*

*Rosa was prepared for 100 per cent of her remaining classes for the term!*

The penultimate step is to conduct periodic accuracy checks to make sure that the student's self-monitoring is being undertaken accurately. Again, within an adult learning environment we would anticipate that this would be done in an understated way – perhaps checking in with the student and asking some judicious questions about how they are progressing with their goals.

The final step is to fade the monitoring plan, and, along with positive feedback, it is vital for the attainment of academic independence (Hattie and Timperley, 2007). When students begin to see sustained success, they are likely to understand that the processes in place work, and need fewer reminders to employ them. Students on the spectrum, however, may find that 'mindblindness' and/or problems with executive function and working memory mean that they require reminders to transfer processes or skills from one context to another. Sometimes asking the question, 'what have you tried in the past that has worked?' is enough to trigger the student's understanding that old strategies can be used in new contexts. At other times, a more substantial intervention is required.

### Rosa

*The quality of Rosa's work was outstanding, but her confidence remained low for the first few years of her degree. Almost every semester, she would become stuck in a perfectionism-procrastination loop, and would need to be encouraged by the Learning Development Lecturer to hand in something, even if it was incomplete, as she would request – and receive, owing to her health conditions – extension upon extension, until finally, in some semesters, she would reach the very final day when marks could be processed.*

*The only two subjects Rosa ever failed were subjects where, by the time she got to the final extension, the Learning Development Lecturer was on leave. At the start of the next semester when we debriefed and discussed the importance of handing in something in order to get some marks, she would recall that we had used the strategy successfully in the past, but when she was anxious, she could not remember it independently.*

*One assignment was submitted at midnight on the final possible day, after her Counsellor sent her emails every two hours, asking how she was going and requesting an updated draft. In this way, Rosa did not fall into the kind of stasis that can occur when one realises that a hoped-for standard is unlikely to be met; instead, she was encouraged that she was on the right track and just needed to keep going. When she was feeling less anxious, Rosa was able to do this for herself on some occasions, and on others, to recognise that it was time to send an email to a staff member asking what she should do next. This suggested that the monitoring skills were gradually becoming internalised.*

Self-monitoring leads to improved awareness of one's own behaviour (Stasolla, Perilli and Daniani, 2014). The ability to regulate emotions and behaviour is closely linked with the ability to monitor progress towards a goal (Henderson *et al.*, 2015). In self-monitoring, scaffolded activities are designed that create metacognition around on-task and off-task (or productive and unproductive) behaviour. Increased awareness of productive behaviours should lead to the ability to employ such strategies autonomously (Stasolla, Perilli and Daniani, 2014). As we have seen, students on the spectrum may display issues around inhibition (or a lack thereof) and shifting tasks may lead to inappropriate classroom behaviour. As adult learners, they are required to learn and adhere to often implicit or opaque classroom codes of behaviour, which they ultimately must self-monitor. They may also experience difficulties around organisation and working memory, meaning that it may be difficult to complete sub-tasks of their own volition; therefore, there is also a series of academic skills that will require self-monitoring.

In primary and secondary schools, scaffolded self-monitoring activities will typically take the form of students being prompted at set time intervals to record whether they are on or off task. The students then plot a graph of these results to see patterns in their own behaviour (Cleary and Zimmerman, 2004; Draper Rodriguez, Strnadova and Cumming, 2013). Video modelling is also sometimes used to remind students of what the target behaviours look like in the first instance. Modelling or observational learning has been used as an effective classroom intervention for more than 40 years. Based on Albert Bandura's social learning theory, which posits that observing a model of behaviour is an effective means of learning appropriate behaviour (Bandura, 1977; Bellini, Akullian and Hopf, 2007), video modelling introduces modern technology as a means of having 'models' who are very close in age and social standing to the learner. Adult learners in university classrooms may find that there are social cues they can mimic from watching the behaviours of their peers.

The risk with performance monitoring of people on the spectrum is that many are hypersensitive to errors, meaning that offering corrective feedback and identifying or highlighting errors can be interpreted as threatening. Yet, video self-monitoring allows for the student to learn the desired behaviour, have it recorded, and then use the self as the model (Draper Rodriguez, Strnadova and Cumming, 2013; Stasolla, Perilli and Daniani, 2014). Typically, a teacher will support this process by editing out mistakes or distractions so that the student has only the desired behaviours to follow. This reinforces to the student that she or he is capable of demonstrating the preferred behaviour, and creates a positive feedback loop that ultimately develops higher-order cognitive processes that allow students to monitor their own progress (Henderson *et al.*, 2015), processes that may not develop naturally in individuals on the spectrum because of their unusual thought patterns and tendency towards weak central coherence.

### Barry and Troy

*Barry and Troy, two students with Autism Spectrum Disorder, were enrolled in the final year of the Bachelor of Engineering Degree (400 level). The course required that students undertake an independent research project and write a 15,000-word thesis (dissertation) about their project. They were also required to undertake an oral presentation (viva) about their project, with the audience consisting of all other students in the course (approximately 150 students), their own academic supervisor, members of local engineering-related businesses (who were also prospective employers), all other academic staff, who were themselves supervising students, and other senior members of the faculty. The presentation contributed 25 per cent of the final mark for the subject. The oral presentation task was both an academic challenge and a time of considerable stress and angst for all students.*

*In order to prepare the students, I offered to video them over successive rehearsals and to support their development of appropriate strategies and skills to undertake the task. The videos were reviewed, first by themselves, and then with me. They were able to identify elements (levels of information and aspects of performance) that they wished to improve, and I rehearsed them in this process. Both students successfully completed the oral presentation task and both were awarded Distinction grades.*

Self-monitoring also allows students to become aware of any unwanted behavioural mannerisms. One of the symptoms of Autism Spectrum Disorder is the employment of restricted or repetitive behaviours (American Psychiatric Association, 2013). These may take the form of rigid motor mannerisms, known as self-stimulatory behaviours or 'stims', that denote high emotion

– be it excitement, happiness or frustration – in the individual on the spectrum (Attwood, 2007; Kuder, 2013; Sansosti and Powell-Smith, 2010).

### Barry

*Barry, one of the students who engaged in the video self-monitoring rehearsal process, had a particularly annoying 'stim', wherein, while giving his presentation, he would constantly check (every few seconds) with his little finger that his trouser fly was still done up. The self-monitoring exercise allowed him to identify his stim (he indicated embarrassment) and discussion with me allowed him to develop a strategy to overcome it. I asked him to hold an A4 sheet summarising his notes in the hand that he had used to check his fly. This occupied his hand, provided him with an easy-to-read summary as a prompt, and removed the stim.*

Specialised products such as the *MotivAider* are also used in school settings. This is a pager-like device that vibrates at set intervals to remind the student to assess whether she or he is still on task and demonstrating desirable behaviour. The time increments can then be extended in order to fade reminders. Similar processes could be established using existing portable technology such as smart watches or phones while in silent mode. Indeed, the developers of the *MotivAider* have now released an app version featuring some of the functionality of the stand-alone device (Ganz, Heath, Davis and Vannest, 2013).

While in the school setting the focus is often on pro-social skills development, the same principles have also been found to work in increasing on-task behaviour, which assists academic endeavours (Ganz, Heath, Davis and Vannest, 2013) and is critical for those with working memory, task analysis and time-management issues. For some university students on the spectrum, self-monitoring processes may need to be embedded into the kinds of planning and strategising discussed in the previous chapter. Writing a study plan is not enough; students must also develop means of adhering to the plan and being alerted if they are in danger of veering off course. In the learning environment of the university or college, it is extremely unlikely that teaching or support staff would direct students to plot a graph of their on-task behaviour or assist with setting up video-modelling; nor would either activity be particularly socially viable. Given the proliferation of smart phones, tablets, technology-integrated watches and laptops in university classrooms, however, it is possible for students to utilise everyday technology in order to monitor their own learning behaviours. It is important to realise that 'self-monitoring' is not a stand-alone skill (Stasolla, Perilli and Daniani, 2014), but, rather, requires weaving together a number of processes in ways that meet the needs of individual students (Finn, Ramasay, Dukes and Scott, 2015); therefore, a certain amount of trial and error may be involved (Light and McNaughton, 2013). It is also important to acknowledge the importance of self-determination: if the student is to adopt, maintain or generalise particular strategies to facilitate academic success, they will need to choose strategies with which they feel comfortable to engage, rather than those dictated by an academic advisor.

Self-monitoring is a strategy that is often used by neurotypical adolescents and adults, often around behaviours related to eating, exercise or sleep. As such, it is a low – or no – cost option with no social stigma that requires only minimal support, as opposed to specialised training (Ganz, Heath, Davis and Vannest, 2013). There is a need for caution, however; youth on the spectrum appear to be vulnerable to internalising problems as a result of their diminished ability to monitor their own and others' behaviour, and this sensitivity has been linked to the high levels of comorbidity between Autism Spectrum Disorder, anxiety and depression (Attwood, 2007; Henderson *et al.*, 2015).

Numerous books can offer students advice on strategies to use (Freedman, 2010; Harpur, Lawlor and Fitzgerald, 2004; Martin, 2011; Wolf, Thierfeld Brown and Kukiela Bork, 2009), but arguably one of the best in terms of assisting students to generalise and maintain study strategies is Stella Cottrell's *Study Skills Handbook* (Cottrell, 2003), an illustrated guide that includes priority organisers, different note-taking styles (many of them visual), opportunities to backwards-map sub-tasks and, critically, self-evaluation pages for student use. Representing tasks, sub-tasks or schedules graphically, as we have seen in Chapter 4, reduces cognitive load and thus assists students to focus. Another useful low-tech strategy is to print off tasks or assignments on different coloured sheets of paper, in the order that they need to be completed rather than by subject (Riffel, 2008).

## Technology-based strategies

Over the past several years, we have seen the amount of personal technology being used by students in classrooms increase seemingly exponentially. Devices such as laptops, tablets and mobile phones are lightweight, portable, and have readily available add-ons, such as cases, software and apps that make them customisable. This allows students with disabilities to unobtrusively use assistive technologies embedded into devices that are non-stigmatising (Cumming, Strnadova and Singh, 2014; King, 2011; King *et al.*, 2014; Robillard *et al.*, 2013; Servilio and Mazzone, 2012). Mobile devices can be loaded with visual behaviour charts that monitor on-task behaviour (*iReward, GoalTracker*), focus apps (*Pomodoro*), organisational and scheduling apps (*Calendars 5, Wunderlist*), note-taking apps (*AudioNote, SuperNote*) and speech-to-text apps (*Dragon Naturally Speaking*) or text-to-speech apps (*Natural Readers*), which offer students opportunities to support their learning needs and monitor which of their learning behaviours are most productive.

### *Michael*

*Michael is a student in his early twenties at a regional university. He matriculated in 2011 with an Australian Tertiary Admission Rank (ATAR) in the top 30 per cent of the state, but withdrew and took an 18-month leave of absence after not doing well in his first semester of study.*

*Michael appears to be of above-average intelligence but has diagnosed learning difficulties, including dyslexia, along with symptoms of Attention Deficit Hyperactivity (for which he takes medication) and Autism Spectrum Disorder. Reports provided to his Disability Liaison Officer show that he has superior verbal intelligence but reduced working memory and processing speeds. He is often late to class and appointments, and sometimes does not attend at all. At other times, he will just 'pop in' without an appointment. The quality of his assignment work is good, but he has a history of submitting assignments late and attracting penalties for doing so.*

Michael is a prime example of a student with significant ability, who has not yet learned how to internalise and generalise strategies that will assist with his executive function. During consultations, it quickly became apparent that Michael was quite reliant on mobile technology, which is, after all, a socially valid form of assistive technology, commonly used by his peers. He could use mobile phone applications to attempt to organise himself and his thinking, without drawing attention to his disabilities, since his peer group are also typically quite reliant on phones and likely to be using them for entertainment, music, communication or organisation. There was potential to add a suite of apps that would allow him to better develop his academic skills and strategies, and later, to monitor his application of these.

Michael reported that in addition to his issues around executive function, there were some academic language and learning issues. He said that he was having problems understanding lectures, and that he found developing structure, cohesion and an appropriate style in his assessment work to be difficult. Exam preparation and strategies were also problematic. It was suggested to him that he might like to use websites, such as *Readability*, that declutters webpages, or *Natural Reader*, that converts text to speech, to assist with the cognitive load of lectures and readings. *Wunderlist* was recommended for doing task analysis and checking that he was on track to meet the goals he established.

Michael also noted that he had been trying the *Pomodoro* or kitchen timer technique, which is based on the idea that most people can do any task, no matter how unrewarding, for 15 minutes, and that sometimes aiming for and achieving a 15-minute block of focus on a particular activity will lead to working longer. While Michael found the technique both attractive and useful, he had not been able to remember to use it consistently. Michael was then directed to a *Pomodoro* app, which meant that the strategy became more portable than using the oven timer at home, and he was therefore likely to have more opportunities to apply a strategy that he liked and felt was working. He rejected outright the idea of using paper-based assistive technologies, such as traditional diaries and wall calendars, saying that he would not use them. Michael had a key role in deciding which self-monitoring supports would be put in place. The Learning Development Lecturer's role was to apprise him of the options, offer support, and check in with him at key points in the semester to see if the strategies were working effectively. Email prompts were sent to him at key points in the semester (start, mid-way and end) to check on his progress and remind him that assessment tasks were likely to be due. Teaching appointments were supplemented with email support and online consultations, where appropriate.

### Michael

*Michael reported via email that he had been keeping up with classwork, but admitted that he would 'need to be more organised' if he were to 'take on a bigger workload' in future semesters. This was a significant, motivating factor as Michael was on a reduced load in his first year.*

*Michael also used his considerable charm and the facts that he was registered with Disability Services and had been furnished with a 'Reasonable Adjustment' document to negotiate an extension, even though extensions were not one of the agreed adjustments for him.*

Michael is already functionally communicative and literate; his issues lie in understanding, interpreting and recreating disciplinary language. Although this is certainly a concern for many students transitioning to tertiary studies, it is a process made more complex by his auditory processing issues, attention problems and dyslexia. Accordingly, Michael needed to be made aware of metacognitive processes around memory, information retention and genre-specific conventions, and to be explicitly taught the new vocabulary and skills required for his studies (Kuder, 2013). He needed to operate within what Vygotsky titled the Zone of Proximal Development (see Chapter 2), since he was still operating at the first stage of internalisation, 'where performance is assisted by more capable others' (Gallimore and Tharp, 1990, p. 185).

Within the office space, Michael showed significant problems with attention and displayed behaviours (such as pacing, walking around the room, standing beside the lecturer, eating and drinking) that many lecturers might find off-putting or even disrespectful. It is commonly thought that this is an issue of distractability; more accurately, it is a problem with attending. A student with these kinds of issues will be paying too much attention to a particular focus, and then rapidly moving on to another one, and needs to learn how to divide and focus attention on a prioritised task.

Interestingly, when observed within a traditional lecture space, he sat quietly in his seat, waited with his hand up to contribute (and the contribution was meaningful) and generally conformed to expectations about student behaviour in a university classroom. This suggests that Michael had learned the conventions of classroom behaviour and was capable of adhering to them. From a Vygotskian perspective, Michael was operating on the third stage of internalisation within the learning environment of the lecture theatre, 'where performance is developed, automati[s]ed, and fossili[s]ed' (Gallimore and Tharp, 1990, p. 185). Still needing assistance to behave appropriately professional in a staff office may suggest that the effort to conform in class represented an increased cognitive load that he was unable to maintain consistently.

However, it is also the case that spaces where staff were aware of his diagnosis, such as the office in Learning Development, were arguably 'safer' places to behave in a symptomatic manner.

### Donna

*Donna confided that she sometimes 'fakes human emotion', and has learned that a 'good hug gets you out of anything'.*
*She paused, then added: 'But I don't fake it with you.'*

Self-monitoring – for all of us – typically involves a great deal of trial and error. If you are aware that a student is working hard to generalise study strategies, it may be worth instigating some form of check-in process in order to see how they are going. Students on the spectrum, as we have seen in Chapter 4, have a propensity to persist with something, even if it is clearly not working; sometimes it takes a teacher or peer to point out that the strategy needs to be revised or abandoned.

Michael received regular emails from Learning Development asking how he was going with his studies during his first full year at university. Additionally, he would sometimes initiate contact with the Learning Development Lecturer when he realised that assessments were imminent. Because of Michael's erratic time management skills, these contacts typically resulted in appointments, but not always in his attendance at the same. In other words, early monitoring of the new learning and study strategies were, to some degree, monitored externally, with this support being gradually withdrawn as Michael became more reliably able to meet deadlines and he began to see a resultant improvement in his marks.

Michael was quick to implement the *Pomodoro* technique, with which he had already been experimenting. As outlined above, it involves setting a timer for a nominated period of time (typically, 15 minutes) and committing to a task for that concentrated period of time. Having overcome the threat of procrastination involved in *starting* the task, some people will then continue.

### Rosa

*Rosa complained that she did not like the* Pomodoro *technique because just when she was 'getting into the swing of things' the buzzer went off and she had to stop!*

*I re-explained to Rosa that the idea of the strategy is to start something, and that if you wish to continue, that's allowed.*

*She thought on this further, and decided that she would reset the timer to 30-minute intervals instead.*

Some academic staff, who are required to produce and publish papers on their research, also use the *Pomodoro* approach or a modified *Pomodoro* approach. Some use time-based and task-based motivation to improve their attention to the task of writing, which is not enjoyable for all people all the time. For instance, allowing time for a relaxing activity, such as swimming, walking, or having a coffee with colleagues, when – and only when – they have spent a previously determined time on their writing task. We have been told of others who write while their least favourite shows are on television. Having engaged with the task, the hope is that the writer will keep writing after the period (of the show) has ended. Another variation on the theme is the *Write or Die* software, which should only be introduced to students on the spectrum with a comment about the alarming title being something of a pun around 'deadlines'. The software can be customised to reward (by showing kittens or puppies and making soothing noises, such as purring) writing goals, or using disincentives (the screen turning an increasingly violent shade of red, spiders running across the screen, or a discordant alarm sounding) when the goals are not being met. These techniques are easy to relate to students on the spectrum and are particularly helpful not only for assisting them to self-monitor their progress, but also in offering reassurance that writing can be a tiresome task for anyone, regardless of life stage, career, or placement on the Autism Spectrum (or not).

Michael was also keen to use *Wunderlist* to prioritise his learning and study activities and to maintain control over his schedule and deadlines. As we have seen in Chapter 4, students with organisational problems may misplace assignments and materials, not allow enough time, and not know when assignments are due (Cohen and Spenciner, 2011). The *Wunderlist* app is an online to-do list that synchronises across devices, and allows users to categorise tasks in labelled folders. Students can establish folders for each subject being undertaken, yet also see a folder for a particular week, which allows them to forward plan across subjects. There is capacity to set deadlines and recurring deadlines; to share tasks with others via a Dropbox system; to identify subtasks; and to 'star' important or urgent items. Alerts can be seen from the home screen on days when a task is due. Completed tasks are hidden once crossed off, but are archived and can be accessed later if required. In a university or college setting, where most students now carry phones and/or tablets, the app is likely to be socially acceptable and is much more likely to be used than a traditional student diary.

*Wunderlist* has the functionality to set both visual and/or aural reminders. The use of visual schedules and organisers and the explicit teaching of self-regulation strategies can be useful for students with executive function difficulties. As Lauren Riffel argues, many learners, 'whether they have A[ttention] D[eficit] H[yperactivity] D[isorder], L[earning] D[isabilities] or autism for that matter, think in pictures' (Riffel, 2008, p. 9). Michael self-identified as a strongly visual learner, but he knew from his experimentation with *Pomodoro* that aural reminders also worked for him and he felt that using two systems with this shared feature would be beneficial, which it certainly appeared to be.

## Conclusion

Time-management and project-planning strategies are vital for students to succeed, and arguably more so for students on the spectrum, who may have problems with global processing and planning. We can reasonably expect that this particular cohort, who, as we have seen, sometimes have problems with rigid thinking and social codes, may require some time and support in order to internalise these strategies and be confident to apply them across a range of contexts and subjects.

## Tips for Teachers

- Remember that there are differences between 'can't', 'won't' and 'not quite ready yet'. Be patient.

- Students on the spectrum may need more reminders about the kinds of strategies to use than their neurotypical peers, and take more time to generalise them. Be supportive of their endeavours, and resist any temptation to remind the student that you have given similar advice previously.

- Try not to make 'public examples' of students using mobile phones or tablets in class. They may not actually be off task but, rather, attempting to remain on task! Make your policy about mobile phones and other portable devices clear at the start of the semester, and ask students to come and consult with you privately if they have a genuine reason why they need to have alternative access.

- You may need to explain information or strategies more than once. This is not because the students are not trying, not listening or not paying attention (usually!); it is because they are likely to have problems with processing and retrieving information, as well as knowing when it is appropriate to apply a strategy from one context to another, and when it is not (remember 'Foolish Jack Syndrome'!).

# Tips for Learners

- Think about your strengths and evaluate strategies that might work for you.

- Enlist the help of others in learning how to monitor behaviour until you establish *self*-monitoring.

- Take cues about behaviour from your peers, but not necessarily when deciding how or when to start an assignment. Different students learn at different speeds, so allocate yourself enough time to do each of the sub-tasks you identify. Allow for any processing difficulties you may have – for example, if you are a strongly visual learner but your lectures are long, recorded monologues with very few visual slides, you know that the information might be more difficult to process, apply and retain. Allocate extra time not only for the lectures, but also for making some compensatory notes – for example, a mind map that converts the information into a visual format that makes sense to you.

- Identify self-monitoring scaffolds (forms, apps, charts) that you think will work for you. If you are having problems starting or maintaining your system, enlist the help of Disability Support staff, staff from the Learning or Writing centre, or a friendly academic who would be willing to 'check in' with you until the process becomes more automatic.

- Persist. Many people give up on study timetables or other organisational systems the first time that they realise they have done something other than what was planned. Rather than giving up on the plan, adjust it, or ask someone to help you reassess whether it needs adjustment, or whether it is just not the right option for you and your learning style. If the first thing you try does not work for you, keep looking until you find something that does.

# Chapter 7

# Central Coherence

## Introduction

There are several theories about what autism is and what causes it, neurologically speaking. Different theories have suggested that different parts of the brain (including the frontal lobes, amygdala, hippocampus and brain stem) are structurally or functionally different in people with Autism Spectrum Disorder (Kuder, 2013); still other studies have implicated neurochemistry, investigating the efficacy of chemicals such as serotonin in brains of people with Autism Spectrum Disorder (Kuder, 2013). While none of these studies have proven to be conclusive, what does seem clear is that there is a significant genetic basis for the disorder (Kuder, 2013). This means that many on the spectrum are unaware that their thought processes are unusual until they enter formal schooling, since there may well be other members of the household with the same world views and ways of thinking. One way of explaining 'autistic thinking' (Grandin, 2013) is the theory of central coherence.

Central coherence is the ability to synthesise disparate pieces of information, perhaps drawn from different sources, experiences and schemata, both internal and external, to determine a global, higher, more insightful or *gestalt* meaning. Strong central coherence utilises sophisticated mental organising strategies, such as categories, prototypes and schemata, rather than low-level thinking that is literal, tied to the 'concrete' and does not require the use of organising strategies (Norris, 2014, p. 270). Central coherence relies on episodic thinking in order to construct personal meaning from episodic thinking, abstract and conceptual understanding, and context-laden memories (Tulving, 2002).

People with Autism Spectrum Disorder often have difficulty with or have 'weak' central coherence, which can be thought of as difficulty in 'getting the point, or gist', of things; a problem with focusing on *both* the details and the whole or in utilising details to make a meaningful whole. Another way of describing weak central coherence is as 'local' or 'bottom-up' processing rather than 'global' or 'top-down' processing (Neuman, Spezio, Piven and Adolphs, 2006), which refers to the way in which individuals undertake the process of perception. Top-down processing involves pattern recognition from contextual information, such as the brain being able to perceive the meaning of a paragraph due to the context provided by surrounding paragraphs. On the other hand, bottom-up processing begins at the stimulus, for example, the meaning of a paragraph relying on the individual, decontextualised, words used.

The transition to university or college is likely to require strong central coherence, in that students are required to very quickly transition to a new social and educational environment. Challenges include managing academic expectations, and, for those who have moved away from home to study, sharing small living quarters and taking care of personal needs such as banking, cooking and shopping (Adreon and Durocher, 2007; Martino McCarty, 2012). If students have moved away from home to study, they will also have to learn about their new town; where the library is, where the shops are, when, how and when to socialise in a way that is not overly stressful, and all without the familiar comforts of home and established support systems. Navigating this situation is likely to require strong central coherence, but students on the spectrum are more prone to focusing on smaller tasks in great detail, which may make the transition more difficult.

The language and communication difficulties often present within the disorder include a failure to adjust language production to context; a tendency to initiate conversations because of their interest to the speaker (without regard for the listener); selecting socially inappropriate topics of conversation (such as asking someone their weight or age, or, as we saw with James in Chapter 3, making sexually explicit remarks in a teaching environment); difficulty understanding non-literal language; and abruptly shifting conversational topics (Kuder, 2013). All of these traits can be explained in terms of central coherence theory: that the focus is on the text, rather than context; that the speaker is interested in the details of the conversation, without regard for the conversation as a process requiring give-and-take; being unaware of social mores or unwritten codes of behaviour; focusing on the detail and not understanding the removed, implied, non-literal meaning; or deciding that a topic of conversation is complete and not having the social skills to be able to close it off politely. Each of these issues, as we have seen, can lead to breaches of classroom codes of conduct, be they implicit or explicit. Essentially, bottom-up processing or weak central coherence leads to the kind of executive dysfunction we discussed in Chapter 5, and also manifests most particularly in problem-solving scenarios. Temple Grandin sees problem solving as training the brain to be organised, breaking tasks into sequences, relating parts to a whole, staying on task and experiencing accomplishment (Grandin, 2008).

Even though people on the spectrum might like things to be orderly, for others organisation can prove to be a major problem, requiring significant compensatory training. This typically manifests in one of two ways: some students, like Esther (introduced in Chapter 2), will have an organisation 'system' that consists of 'put everything in the bag/folder'. Sorting information according to subject or topic is a task that is delayed, sometimes permanently. This occurs when there is a 'disconnect' between receiving and learning information, and recognising that it may need to be filed or stored for retrieval at another time. Someone with well-developed top-down processing is able to see that storing learned information or materials for future use is part of the same bigger task as learning it in the first place (that is, meeting particular subject outcomes by demonstrating that the content has been learned and can be reviewed, retrieved and applied at a later date or in another situation). For those with a tendency towards bottom-up processing, however, 'learning' and 'filing' remain two separate and unrelated tasks.

The second way in which disorganisation can manifest is as *over*-organisation, related to the procrastination-perfectionism loop we discussed in Chapter 6. Some students may spend enormous amounts of time cleaning and organising their desk or study space – or indeed, the entire house – because they are focused on the bottom-up task (organising oneself preparatory to study), rather than the global task of getting the study done (which would typically involve being just organised *enough* to be productive). Most neurotypical students leave the major clean-up until after the task is completed, but a student on the spectrum who becomes focused on the process of getting organised to study may become totally focused on completing that activity to a high standard, rather than thinking about the meta-activity of doing the study that is required in the time that is left.

### Kate

*Kate was in the final stages of her PhD studies and was expected to show a final draft of a chapter to her supervisors in a few days. She allocated two days at home to work towards this goal, promising herself that she would 'clear the desk' as the first point of order.*

*When her partner arrived home from work on the first day, he eyed the gleaming, cobweb-free house, polished furniture, spotless oven and streak-free windows inside and out of the entire house and asked, 'so what's due, then?' Clearing the desk in order to start work had become cleaning the room, and then cleaning the house, and had subsumed the time allocated for studying in said clean space.*

Breaking things into sequences is another example of top-down processing, and one with which some people on the spectrum may have difficulty. As we discussed in Chapter 5, many students require assistance to undertake task analysis and then prioritise the sub-tasks; further, they may require scaffolded assistance to begin to self-regulate these activities, as we have seen in Chapter 6. Yet, we also know, as Grandin suggests, that this is a skill that can be learned; after all, many people on the spectrum are drawn to STEM (Martino McCarty, 2012), and Engineering, for one, is all about problem solving via task sequencing.

### Kate

*Kate has renovated three properties, doing much of the work herself and project-managing all three. Over time, she has created a master list of tasks that typically need to be done, and the order in which they will be completed (for example: tear up the old carpet; prepare and paint the ceilings, then do the walls and finally lay the floor. This standard task master list means that any paint from the ceiling that drips will not do so onto the new wall paint, and any that falls on the floor will later be covered, negating the need for dropsheets).*

*When there are new problems to be solved or tasks to be prioritised, she creates a new sequence list, and then asks her father, who is a qualified and experienced engineer, to check it. There are times when she rings and lists the things that need to happen, and asks are there any issues or 'traps for new players' of which she needs to be aware (for example, that a plumber might need to be on site to move the gas point when new flooring is being laid, since the height of the floor might change marginally). He has also given her some key phrases to use with tradespeople when things deviate from the plan (for example, 'what will it take to keep the job moving?').*

*While coping with the details of this, Kate typically sends the family away to visit other family. Trying to manage the project at hand, as well as manage the global logistics of family life, is too much to deal with simultaneously. She has two good friends within a two-hour radius on whom she can call if she is feeling overwhelmed or having a meltdown – both have rearranged their own plans and cheerfully arrived to stay on a worksite and help when Kate has been in mid-project meltdown because the master plan and agreed sequence have gone awry.*

As we can see above, a person with a preference for bottom-up or details-oriented processing can, indeed, learn to apply scaffolds that accommodate global, bigger-picture thinking; however, it is likely that they will still find it stressful to do so, and require support and understanding from those around them.

As we have seen, the relationship between the parts of the whole can be problematic for individuals on the spectrum. Uta Frith proposed the *Weak Central Coherence Theory* of autism, wherein a person with strong central coherence, looking at an expanse of trees, would see the forest. A person with weak central coherence would see only many individual trees (Frith, 1989). For Frith, weak central coherence explained both deficits and strengths; why some people on the spectrum have *savant* skills and are able to focus at a very detailed level, seemingly able to discern a minute element from a mass of complex information or data, while at the same time have difficulty in extracting a global meaning (Frith, 1989). While weak central coherence may be easily interpreted in a negative light, as a deficit, Happé and Frith, more recently, have argued that a detail-focused cognitive style can also be seen in a positive light, as a bias rather than as a weakness (Frith and Happé, 1994; Happé and Frith, 2006). As with Theory of Mind and executive function, Lopez, Leekam and Arts argue that central coherence is not a single cohesive construct (Lopez, Leekam and Arts, 2008).

Grandin's final point was about needing to retrain the brain to accommodate the above factors in order to experience accomplishment. This is particularly important because of the tendency towards perfectionism within this cohort, and the high prevalence of anxiety and depression. Students who do not see themselves as achieving commensurate with their abilities are prone to internalise this as 'failure', and this can lead to further social isolation, depression and anxiety. Like any student, those on the spectrum need to celebrate their successes in order to stay motivated.

Laurent Mottron and Sylvie Belleville attempted to explain the phenomenon of weak central coherence by comparing the approach to drawing of a neurotypical professional draftsman with that of an autistic man with exceptional artistic ability (Mottron and Belleville, 1993). They found the autistic man began drawing by selecting a relatively unimportant detail and then adding contiguous elements, whereas the draftsman began by constructing outlines and then filling in the details (Mottron and Belleville, 1993). This would appear to illustrate differences in the top-down/bottom-up approaches to task management; however, caution needs to be exercised in adopting the top-down/bottom-up explanation for strong/weak central coherence. The differences in the two approaches may simply relate to the level of training that the two men underwent – or did not undergo – and cannot be relied upon to point to how we support our students who have Autism Spectrum Disorder.

### Ronaldo

*Ronaldo, a professional draftsman and a skilled artist with high-functioning Autism Spectrum Disorder, studied Architecture at university. When asked how he approached the task of drawing (in relation to the two methods identified by Mottron and Belleville described above), he recounted that: 'There's a method to it; you are taught it at university. First I draw the plan, which has to take account of the direction of best light. Climate affects the orientation of a building. But while I am drawing the plan, I am already thinking about the construction method because it dictates the materials (concrete, brick, etc.) that I will use. While I am thinking about it, I make lists of all the things that are required, because I can't hold it all in my head at once. I concentrate on it, one part at a time. I am envisaging it in 3D – it's not just a flat thing; it consists of spaces. I determine the size of windows and make decisions about ceiling heights, and I draw these on cross-sections. At the end I check off the list to make sure I have covered everything that has been asked for.'*

*When asked whether he employed a different method when drawing a building or a city-scape that already exists, not a plan for a new building, he said: 'First I select an item that is central to the picture and draw an outline. Then I sketch in, roughly, the shapes of other buildings on each side to get the proportions correct. Then I start to fill in the major parts of the details and all the minutiae.'*

Ronaldo *has* – or, perhaps, *has acquired* – strong central coherence, at least in relation to how he approaches the task of drawing. His description of how he does this would appear to be top-down, involving contextual decisions first and maintaining relevance to the context throughout the process (never losing sight of the 'big picture'). This would suggest that top-down thinking can be learned, and it suggests that as university teachers we can have a role in supporting the learning of our students with Autism Spectrum Disorder. Sometimes we do not directly 'teach' the students so much as create the learning environment in which learning takes place.

### Ronaldo

*When pressed on how he learned, Ronaldo said that as well as watching what lecturers did in his drawing class when they drew on the board, [he] learned best from other students in his drawing and design classes. 'In our drawing classes we had our drawing boards side by side and we could talk about what we were doing while we were doing it. It's best when I learn visually.'*

Grandin further explains that prior to training herself in problem solving, she could not 'hold one piece of information in [her] mind while [she] manipulate[d] the next step in the sequence' (Grandin, 2013, p. 145). We have already seen that task analysis, visual reminders and checklists work for project planning, time management and self-monitoring. They can similarly be applied to problem solving, since the issues relate not so much to the kinds of tasks, as to the symptomatic behaviours of the students on the spectrum. In Ronaldo's case, he has created a series of checklists to compensate, that have been internalised and generalised over time.

In Chapter 4 we discussed the types of learning experiences to which university students are exposed, in particular, experiences that require the ability to: deduce and abstract meaning; to establish relationships between parts of subject matter and real situations; to hypothesise and theorise; and to test these against reality. This process involves questioning and reframing knowledge through a process of synthesis and development of new knowledge (Gluck and Draisma, 1997), a process that can be difficult for people with weak central coherence, who may have a heightened focus on details that overrides their focus on the whole. The inability to hold information in mind in order to use it later in other tasks can leave students vulnerable to misinterpreting assessment tasks, situations and communications.

## Central coherence and interpretation of assessment tasks

Since central coherence is the ability to focus on details as well as 'wholes', it allows us to understand contexts and to relate 'parts' to each other. Those with weak central coherence may have difficulty seeing connections and making generalisations, and in prioritising and choosing. They may also demonstrate inattentiveness to new tasks and have a preference for the known (Cumine, Leach and Stevenson, 1998). For university students on the spectrum, this presents a problem. As we identified in Chapter 4, university learning focuses on developing 'higher-order' thinking skills (Anderson,

Krathwohl and Bloom, 2001), rather than solely asking students to remember and reproduce what has been learned. It involves analytical learning (Ballard and Clanchy, 1991) and requires that students be able to deduce and abstract meaning and establish relationships between parts of subject matter and real situations. It teaches students to hypothesise and theorise and to test these against reality in a process that involves whether they can question and reframe knowledge; a process of synthesis and development of new knowledge (Gluck and Draisma, 1997). University learning requires that students move beyond the known to the unknown.

Assessment questions do not occur in isolation from a context. Indeed, they occur within multiple layers of context that form the hidden curriculum and that need to be understood by those who attempt to answer them. Assessment questions are set to examine to what extent the student has understood the subject content, and may relate to a particular aspect or sub-aspect of a subject (such as a particular theoretical, philosophical, methodological or scientific approach). That subject relates to the sub-discipline (for example, a subject on Hydraulics forms part of the sub-discipline of Mechanical Engineering), and the sub-discipline occurs within the context of the discipline, such as Mechanical Engineering being part of the discipline of Engineering. If the Hydraulics subject were part of the sub-discipline of Mechatronics, then the assessment question would likely require reference to robotics. Figure 7.1 illustrates the multiple contexts to which assessment questions relate.

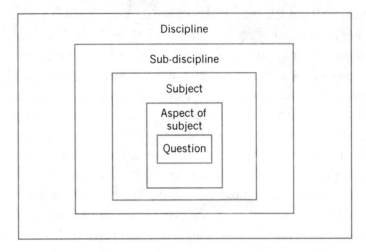

**Figure 7.1: Contextualisation of assessment questions**

When students attempt to answer assessment questions, they need to recognise how the question is embedded within the layers of both the explicitly taught curriculum and the hidden curriculum. For example, a question may occur within a subject on Australian or American History. The student should recognise the approach taken in the subject (for example, has it been taught from a social history, economic history, feminist history or military history perspective?) and 'decode' the question and respond to it in relation to the approach taken. If it were a subject taught within the discipline of Education, then it may form part of a professional qualification, and may be seeking an answer that responds to the practical application of teaching. Similarly, if it were a legal or ethical question occurring within the Faculty of Nursing or Faculty of Medicine, then the answer is likely to need to refer to the legal or ethical application within those professions, rather than simply unpacking the point of Law. It is insufficient for students to answer assessment questions as though they had occurred in isolation from those layered contexts, since to do so would leave open the potential for 'not answering the question' or more accurately, not answering the implied aspects of the question, as well as the stated aspects. This is one aspect of what we mean by relating 'parts to each other' and relating 'parts to wholes' within the academic learning context. Since those with weak central coherence may have difficulty identifying and understanding the layered connections of subject matter and assessment tasks, or may not 'attend' to the implied contextual layers because of their preference for the 'known', 'stated' and 'obvious', then it is important that we make these explicit when we can. Understandably, under examination conditions it would not be appropriate to 'unpack' questions to such an extent that they lost their capacity to test a student's understanding; however, it is appropriate when discussing assessment tasks within the classroom setting to canvass the layers of meaning within the question. After all, we are teaching students not only about subject content, but how to approach that content, and how to think about that content within a contextual framework.

Most teachers, including university and college academics, can recall instances where students have provided literal – or, seemingly, flippant – responses to assessment tasks, in particular under examination conditions. Thanks to the internet, the kinds of answers that once only teachers found amusing can now be shared more broadly. Examples that are commonly known include the response, 'There it is!' when asked to find $x$ in Mathematics; 'At the bottom of the page', when asked in American History, 'Where was the Declaration of Independence signed?'; or in response to a Physics question asking how you can lift an elephant with one hand, the biologically-focused response: 'You can never find an elephant with one hand, in order to lift it.'

Students on the spectrum may inadvertently do the same thing; not for amusement or because they do not understand the content, but because they have been unable to work out the layered contexts in order. Their teachers, however, may become frustrated or even a little angry. After all, a great deal of time has been spent teaching the content and then setting the assessment task or preparing the examination paper, and these answers appear to mock that process. Consider the History essay question: '"World War II saw many people question old beliefs *and* argue for change."

To what extent do you agree?' (Government of Victoria, n.d.). In order to understand what it is that the marker wants the candidate to demonstrate, the student must understand not only that this is a 'double-barrelled' question – about old beliefs *and* arguing for change – but that it refers to the particular time frame of World War II. Further, they must unpack the meaning of the phrase, 'to what extent'. This is a question phrase that many students find difficult, but it is likely to be particularly vexing for students with weak central coherence. Typically, students must make a decision as to whether their argument will be, 'to a great extent', 'to some extent, but there were other factors', 'to some extent, but really, I think the critical social change resulting from World War II was X...'; 'to a small extent', or 'to no extent at all was this true' (the latter, typically, being a difficult case to make). In order to choose the best stance for their argument, the student must first recall all that they know about World War II *as a whole*, and evaluate that in light of the question's central theme of social change. A student with a bottom-up processing style is unlikely to be able to identify the layers of the answer, 'I don't agree at all' or 'I somewhat agree'. If that is largely where the argument ends, the student is likely to fail.

An 'A+' answer to this essay question, however, would first discuss the two issues raised: whether World War II made people question their beliefs; and how their beliefs changed as a result of that questioning. It would then discuss whether questioning old beliefs led people to argue for change. Rather than responding negatively, we perhaps need to consider whether the student who responded literally may be a student with Autism Spectrum Disorder, and hence have weak central coherence; one who was 'seeing the trees', rather than 'the forest'. Effectively, when students with Autism Spectrum Disorder cannot figure out the context in which the question sits or they do not know the subject content required to answer the questions in the way that is expected, they may answer the obvious parts of the question without linking it to what they have already learned.

## Central coherence and the use of schemata

Strong central coherence is the ability to develop and utilise sophisticated mental organising strategies, such as categories and schemata. Students with Autism Spectrum Disorder are likely to have weak central coherence, as we described above, but they may have high level visual-spatial intelligence (Gardner, 1993, 1999). This lends itself to learning through the use of drawings and verbal and physical imagery, including graphics, charts and multi-media. Since students on the spectrum may find it difficult to infer from published texts what they are meant to approximate when they write an essay, it is helpful if they are provided with schemata that give them a guide to the structure that is required.

The schema in Figure 7.2 shows the basic structure of an essay. It consists of several sections: an introduction, three aspects (it could be any number as required to answer the question), each with a mini-conclusion and a final conclusion. Each of the sections may be a paragraph or several paragraphs, depending on the length of the essay that has been set. It may be written linearly – from introduction forwards; or it may be written organically – in no particular order – but placed within a logical, linear framework. In a linear approach, after the research has been done and the writer has sufficient control of the topic, the introduction is written first. The introduction will outline the major elements of the essay and these will be written in the order outlined. The conclusion will draw together the mini-conclusions from each section. In an organic approach, the writing begins when the writer has done sufficient research to have reasonable control over one aspect of the essay. When this is written, it then opens up questions of what to research and write next, or indeed, what needs to be written to get to the current point. Like the linear approach, it is concluded by drawing together ideas from each of the mini-conclusions from each aspect.

This structure has a number of applications. It is useful as the over-arching structure for essays that require comparison, discussion, evaluation and/or analysis, and is suitable for discussions that can be easily thought of as distinct units. It also works as an internal structure for all chapters of theses. The structure divides the essay into themes or 'aspects' and although the diagram shows three aspects, there is no limit to the number possible.

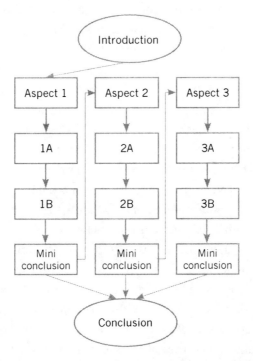

**Figure 7.2: Schema for structure of essays and chapters of theses**

As well as essays, many disciplines require students to write reports. All of the Science disciplines (Natural Sciences, such as Biology, Chemistry, Physics; Earth Sciences, such as Physical Geography; Space Sciences; Sport or Exercise Sciences), Medical Sciences (Medicine, Nursing, Pharmacology), Social Sciences (Psychology, Anthropology, Archaeology, Education, Human Geography, Sociology), Engineering disciplines and many of the Mathematical and Technology disciplines require students to write reports of procedures, practical applications and experiments. The schema in Figure 7.3 shows the basic structure of an experimental report; however, it can be adapted to suit a range of situations that do not involve experiments, such as reports that require narrative accounts or accounts of procedures. In Education or in Nursing, student teachers or nurses can use this structure to report on their practical experiences, such as micro-teaching and guided nursing. For example, a student teacher might report on a small group teaching event: the Introduction would describe what school and what the teaching event aimed to do. The Methods might report on the number of children, their ages, how many girls and boys, and any special characteristics of individuals. It would also describe what was done. Instead of 'Results', there might be 'Outcomes', or indeed this aspect might be blended in with the discussion, but it would focus on what was achieved. The Conclusion sums up the whole experience in light of what was set out to be done.

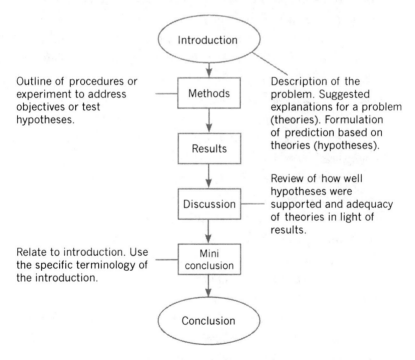

**Figure 7.3: Schema for reports of experiments or narrative account**

Providing students with schemata, such as the ones above, can assist them to better visualise what is required when writing essays and reports for assessment purposes; and since students on the spectrum typically have high visual intelligence and low auditory processing, it makes sense to devise and employ tools that engage their visual intelligence. The schemata provided above are also helpful for those students who are required to write theses or dissertations. Instead of each aspect being a paragraph or a few paragraphs in length (depending on the overall word limit), each aspect would be a chapter, with sub-sections.

### Eric

*Eric had been enrolled, part time, in a PhD in Environmental Engineering for eight years, which exceeded the university's prescribed timeframe for completion. He had done an enormous amount of practical work: several field trials involving planting of crops, computer modelling, statistical modelling and laboratory experiments. His analysis for each experiment, test, model and trial was complete but he was 'swimming' in the data and seemingly unable to write his thesis (dissertation). He was highly anxious and stated that he wanted to withdraw from the programme.*

*Urged to do so by his supervisor, he made an appointment in Learning Development to talk with me about his 'lack of progress'. What became immediately clear was his lack of understanding about how a thesis like his could be structured. I drew on the board various schemata (variants and combinations of the experimental report schema and the essay schema above) and then I assisted him to devise a visual schema of how his thesis could be structured.*

*Six weeks later, Eric submitted his 100,000-word PhD and he graduated a few months later. He told me that the single, most useful, support towards completion of his thesis was our discussion about schemata.*

As well as providing students with visual schemata that describe the common aspects of essays, reports and theses (dissertations), we can also assist them with the vocabulary signals that cue the reader in to what is occurring in a particular part of the essay or report. Many university essays or reports receive low or fail grades, not because they do not contain the correct information, but because the marker is unable to understand what is happening in the writing; the vocabulary 'signals' that alert the reader to what is happening, such as an advancement or a change of direction in the argument, using words such as 'however', 'nevertheless' or 'at the same time', are missing, scrambled or inappropriately used. When the vocabulary signals align with the writer's intent and the flow of the argument, then it is easier for the reader to understand the essay or report and the more likely it is to attract a high mark. Unlike reports, academic essays usually require there to be no sub-headings or visual support materials, so the flow of the argument is largely (perhaps entirely) dependent on the vocabulary signals. Figure 7.4 provides a basic schema for the main vocabulary signals that help readers. There are, of course, many other word signals that writers can use, but these may assist you to discuss with your students the effects that certain words have on the text, the relationship between parts of an argument and the vocabulary items that writers use – and the effect on your understanding and, therefore, on their marks.

| Aspect of writing | Word signals |
|---|---|
| **Description**<br><br>Descriptive ideas that give attributes, specifics or set information about a topic. The main idea is that attributes of a topic are discussed, e.g. who, where, when and how. | for example, which was one, this particular, for instance, specifically, such as, attributes of, that is, namely, properties of, characteristics are, qualities are, marks of, in describing... |
| **Sequence**<br><br>Ideas grouped on the basis of order or time. The main idea is procedure or history related, e.g. recipe procedures, history of civil war battles, growth from birth to 12 months. | afterwards, later, finally, last, early, following, to begin with, to start with, then, as time passed, continuing, to end, years ago, in the first place, before, after, soon, more recently... |
| **Causation**<br><br>Presents causal or cause-and-effect-like relations between ideas. The main idea is organised into cause-and-effect parts, e.g. directions: if you want to take good pictures then you must...; explanations: the idea explained is the effect and the explanation is its cause. | as a result, because, since, for the purpose of, caused, led to, consequence, thus, in order to, this is why, if/then, the reason, so, in explanation, therefore... |
| **Problem/solution**<br><br>The main ideas are organised into two parts: a problem part and a solution part that responds to the problem by trying to eliminate it, or a question part and answer part that reponds to the question by trying to answer it, e.g. scientific articles often first raise a question or problem and then seek to give an answer or solution. | *problem*: problem, question, puzzle, perplexity, enigma, riddle, issue, query, need to prevent, the trouble...<br><br>*solution*: solution, answer, response, reply, rejoinder, return, comeback, to satisfy the problem, to set the issue at rest, to solve these problems... |
| **Comparison**<br><br>Relates ideas on the basis of difference and similarities. The main idea is organised in parts that provide a comparison, contrast or alternative perspective on a topic, e.g. political speeches, particularly where one view is clearly favoured over the other. | not everyone, but, in contrast, all but, instead, act like, however, in comparison, on the other hand, whereas, in opposition, unlike, have in common, share, resemble, the same as, different from, differentiate, compared to, while, although... |

**Listing**

Listing can occur with any of these five aspects. Listing simply groups ideas together. Passages are often organised as a listing of descriptions about a topic. A sequence always contains a listing of ideas, but the ideas are ordered sequentially. A listing can occur when groups of effects are listed, groups of solutions are posted, groups of ideas are contrasted to another idea, and so on.

and, in addition, also, include, moreover, besides, first, second, third etc., subsequent, furthermore, at the same time, another, and so forth...

**Figure 7.4: Basic aspects of writing and the word signals that cue readers to what is happening in the argument**

Another useful schema to assist students is one that describes the usual structure of an academic paragraph; not the introductory or concluding paragraphs, but paragraphs that make up the majority of the essay or report. It consists of three sections: the topic sentence or linked topic sentences; support sentences; and the conclusionary sentence or sentences. Support sentences may be any number and in any combination, but they are intended to provide evidence for what has been stated or claimed in the topic sentence or sentences and to extend the argument.

1. TOPIC SENTENCE...often in the form of a claim or assertion.

2. SUPPORT SENTENCES...these may be:

   - quotation

   - argument

   - statistics

   - examples

   - explanation

   - visuals (collective or illustrative).

3. CONCLUSIONARY SENTENCE(S)...a wrap-up or comment on the above. Sometimes an explicit link to the next paragraph.

Frequently, academic paragraphs utilise a 'firstly', 'secondly', 'lastly' format to draw the reader's attention to the 'moves' in the academic argument being put forth. These moves lexically signal to the reader that something different is about to be provided. It may be an advance in the argument, or even a side-step, but this series of moves are intended to build the depth or argument, overall.

1. TOPIC SENTENCE...in the form of an assertion or claim.

2. EXPANSION

- Firstly...

- Conclusion to first idea.

- Secondly...

- Conclusion to second idea.

3. CONCLUSIONARY SENTENCE(S).

Providing students with schemata, such as those for academic paragraphs and for essay and report structure, allows them to visualise those aspects of academic writing (and hence assessment) that are recognised as valuable within the academy and therefore likely to be rewarded with high grades. Schemata provide a 'fill-in-the-blanks' approach for those students who are wedded to detail at the expense of the 'big-picture'; in essence, they provide a shape for the big picture. The provision of schemata, or discussions about the structural expectations of academic writing tasks, serves to scaffold the learning of all students, not just those on the spectrum.

Once these schemata can be applied on an assignment level, the student will normally come to an understanding of the discipline and its expectations of writers in the discipline.

## Madeleine

*Madeleine is a very good student in Legal Studies. When asked how she had learnt to write high quality essays in the subject, she described what she titled a 'basic platform' for how to write the genre. She said, 'In each paragraph I define, describe, give context, back up ideas, and assess the argument, including points of law. This is my checklist. I get anxious if I can't fill in all the bits in each paragraph. I also have the textbook and the case handouts as models. It [the essay] has to meet my criteria of what it has to be [the checklist]. It's just logical!*

*'There's a point at which you have to come away from your structure and have an understanding of how you feel about the topic, yourself. And you have to look at it from the point of view of the legislators, the law enforcers, the judicial system, the person charged and other people in court, and also how society would look at it. The law sets up consequences that have an overall impact on society. You need to include human factors. You come to the point of explaining and describing through the cases.*

*'At the end you provide an overall analysis. Ask "What does this bring to society? What does it bring to the topic?" The analysis should talk about who it covers and what its impact is.'*

*'It's like a cake,' she said, much to the amusement of the Learning Development Lecturer, who had heard this kind of metaphor before. 'You have to have the objective for the essay – making the cake. Then you add layers of cream to hold it together [the evidence/cases]. The cream can't overpower the cake, but it needs to be there, especially if it's a sponge with five tiers [the checklist], if that metaphor makes sense! But most of all, you need to have understanding.'*

Madeleine has started with a bottom-up processing style (looking at the details required in each paragraph), but has learned the overall shape to the point at which she can seamlessly weave these smaller parts together in more of a top-down processing style using her schema to 'fill in all the bits'. She has read widely within the genre of legal studies and case law, and learned how to apply this style of writing to her own essays. She has internalised the individual elements that make up the structure of each paragraph and the structure of the essay overall. Most of all, she realises that she has to personally engage with the topic, to have – and to demonstrate – 'understanding'.

## Conclusion

This chapter has established that students with Autism Spectrum Disorder, who tend to have weak central coherence and an inclination to be 'bottom-up' thinkers, can nevertheless engage with scaffolded learning in order to produce the required written artefacts that are markers of success in academia. What we need to do as teachers is to provide suitable tools that will support the transition from novice to expert, by creating a positive learning environment and by providing the kinds of scaffolds that are required. We cannot simply teach 'content' and set assessments. This chapter has provided examples of various tools, such as essay and report writing schemata, that can assist you to scaffold student learning.

## Tips for Teachers

- Analyse your own successes in learning and identify times when you have been a top-down or bottom-up learner. What helped you to achieve your success?

- Do not just teach 'content'; scaffold your students' learning so that they can demonstrate what they actually know, including how to write successfully within the discipline.

- Provide quality feedback on student assessments as this is one of the prime opportunities you will have as a teacher to explain to students what is expected.

- Set assessment tasks that relate to the learning outcomes for the subject.

- Never assume that students know how to write an essay or report. Even if they have learned this previously, they may have done so within different contexts. Give them good examples of how it is done within your subject and your discipline. Never give an example of 'what not' to do.

- Consult with Learning Development academics in your institution for support in scaffolding student learning and assessment in your classes.

## Tips for Learners

- Identify whether you are a top-down or bottom-up learner. Do you see the 'whole' or do you naturally focus on the 'parts'?

- If you are a 'bottom-up' learner, devise scaffolds or schemata that start to place the parts into the whole.

- Consult your teachers (lecturer or tutor) to see whether you are adequately covering what is required, or whether you need to adjust what you're doing.

- Read lots of materials within your discipline so that you become familiar with the genre that is required.

- Practise writing using the 'academic paragraph' schema provided in this chapter.

- Allow plenty of time to re-adjust to adopting a 'schema' approach to completion of your written assignments.

- Your institution will have learning support staff available, who are able to offer you advice and feedback on your assessment tasks and how you are approaching them. Allow plenty of time to access that support and avail yourself of this opportunity.

# Chapter 8

# Conclusion

As we have seen, students with Autism Spectrum Disorder may be good candidates for tertiary study; indeed, some of the attributes typically associated with the disorder may prove to be beneficial within the context of higher education. Single-minded determination and unusual interests or perspectives may be advantageous, and those who prefer to study alone in a room are far more likely to succeed than their highly social counterparts who are more committed to experiencing every aspect of university or college life.

Not only do some students on the spectrum find that college or university gives some legitimacy to their interests and preferred work patterns, but for many, behavioural quirks or oddities become more acceptable and the kind of bullying that, sadly, occurs in many school playgrounds and classrooms is likely to be rare. Nevertheless, it is difficult terrain to negotiate. Even for younger students on the spectrum, those who may have been properly diagnosed in childhood or adolescence and received appropriate interventions and support, the process of transition can be overwhelming. The supports and strategies with which they became familiar in infant, primary (elementary) or secondary school are unlikely to be readily available at college or university, and this phenomenon is sometimes referred to as 'ageing out' (Gaus, 2011; Gerhart and Holmes, 2005). This abrupt decrease in structural supports can, in some instances, lead to regression (Gaus, 2011). It is important, therefore, that students are confident to seek help, and that we, as their teachers and representatives of our institutions, position ourselves in such a way that their confidence is not misplaced.

Just as there is no 'one-size-fits-all' approach that will work for all neurotypical students, there is not one that will work for all students on the spectrum. Clearly, given the sizes of some on-campus classes, we will not be able to offer tailored individual support to every student on the spectrum. But just as clearly, we do have a duty of care and an obligation to support all students to success. Negativity from teaching staff and a general lack of sensitivity to the learning preferences of students on the spectrum have been identified as being among the largest areas of concern for college and university students on the spectrum (Garrison-Wade and Lehmann, 2009; Martino McCarty, 2012). Improving these areas is likely to lead to greater success and higher rates of completion for this cohort. In this book we have outlined some of the key areas of concern when teaching students on the spectrum, and endeavoured to explain why their behaviour may follow particular patterns. We have attempted to move beyond merely the 'problem' of defining idiosyncratic behaviours, however, to potential solutions that will help to bridge the gap between the students' ideas about how one studies, and the actual requirements of study.

In the introductory chapter we explained what Autism Spectrum Disorder is, and how it may present in the classroom. The subsequent three chapters examined how the symptoms of the disorder may manifest in terms of classroom behaviours (and misbehaviours). Some students will not understand the inherent requirements of particular disciplines, or have deeply entrenched views of what the discipline 'should' be and why they should be a part of it, even when it is clear that they are not achieving to their potential. Supports to assist the students within the disciplines are important, but facilitating the offering of timely, empathetic, professional career counselling may ultimately prove to be more useful to the student. In addition to this discussion, Chapter 2 points out the sector-, discipline- or subject-specific language that they are expected to understand and apply, particularly with regard to assessment tasks. It also outlines the behavioural codes with which the students are expected to comply, and our obligations to assist them in doing so.

Students on the spectrum will often be very rigid in their thinking, as discussed in Chapter 4, and this can impact on this kind of determination to 'stay the course'. It can also lead to some unusual classroom behaviours, as we have seen in Chapter 3, since students may not be able to self-regulate or adapt their behaviours to suit different learning situations.

The next section of the book dealt with the issues that manifest when there are deficits in working memory and executive function. Again, rigid thinking can lead to some study or revision strategies that are less than helpful when attempting to balance the, at times, seemingly insurmountable pile of deadlines that are typical in a full-time study load. Chapter 5, on Project Planning and Multi-tasking, offers advice on assisting the students to decode what is really expected and plan for success.

Some students, however, will not be able to easily internalise, generalise and maintain the sorts of advice we are suggesting. For these students, you may need to offer some additional support, or at least engage with them as they attempt to self-monitor. In Chapter 6 we discuss simple and unobtrusive ways that students can check their own social and academic behaviours, until such time as they become normalised. Chapter 7 addressed strong and weak central coherence or top-down versus bottom-up processing. As a means of scaffolding students' learning, we provided a number of schematic tools that are designed to support them toward a top-down processing style in relation to assessment tasks.

Chapter 7 focused on central coherence, which in many ways underpins the symptoms and peculiarities of Autism Spectrum

Disorder. A processing method whereby details are noticed in a local or 'bottom-up' manner, rather than more usual global or 'top-down' one, leads to rigid or literal thinking, socially inappropriate conversations or behaviours, and issues around executive function and working memory that manifest in problems with time management, project planning, self-monitoring and understanding class materials and assessments. Students can be taught, however, how to look for other pieces information and eventually, how to see them as part of a larger picture or checklist.

You will have noticed in the various case studies that many decisions around the welfare and academic careers of our students were made in consultation with Disabilities Liaison Officers, Student Support Advisors, Counsellors and faculty staff. A collaborative approach works best since these students may have alternative – and, in some cases, quite idiosyncratic – ways of seeing the world, processing information or communicating with their classmates. As we have noted, some students on the spectrum may need assistance when adjusting to living independently; others may be prone to depression if either the transition or the trajectory of success does not quite go as they had envisaged. Enlist the help and support of other professionals in order to get the best outcomes for your students.

As you read through the case studies, you may have recognised certain characteristics or behaviours that are also present in some of your colleagues. As we suggested at the start of this book, the college or university environment may well be the natural habitat of the person on the spectrum, since it offers a socially acceptable space within which to single-mindedly pursue a niche interest, and to engage in solitary research. Most teaching is monodirectional, and sometimes it can even be pre-recorded and delivered online. Research outcomes are either published, without an immediate audience, or are presented at conferences which have strict guidelines about presentations and questions arising from them. If some of your peers demonstrate some of the qualities we would expect to see in those on the spectrum, there may be times when these behaviours are frustrating. In this case, you will need to extend the same kind of understanding to your colleagues as we do to our students on the spectrum. As with the students, work with the individual, paying close attention to her or his strengths and weaknesses, and try to avoid asking them to do things of which they are not yet capable.

Finally, and most importantly, we would again like to thank our students on the spectrum – not only those whose stories appear within these pages, but all who have come through our doors and shared their unusual views on life with us. Working with this cohort is sometimes challenging, often interesting and mostly rewarding. These are students who – in our experience – are typically very interested in the subject matter, very motivated to do well, very keen to follow rules, and willing to apply the strategies we share (and let us know, sometimes in great detail, when they do not work for them!). They are also largely appreciative of our help.

Don't we wish that all students were like that?

# References

Ackerman, D.S., Gross, B.L., Heisley, D. and Perner, L. (2005) *Nurturing the Special Student: Understanding the Needs of Students with Challenges.* California State University Northridge Scholarworks. Available at www.scholarworks. csun.edu/bitstream/handle/10211.2/1760/AckermanDavid2005_02. pdf?sequence=1, accessed on 22 July 2014.

Adams, M. and Brown, S. (2006) 'Introduction.' In M. Adams and S. Brown (eds) *Towards Inclusive Learning in Higher Education* (pp. 1–9). London and New York: Routledge.

Adreon, D. and Durocher, J. (2007) 'Evaluating the college transition needs of individuals with high-functioning autism spectrum disorders.' *Intervention in School and Clinic 42,* 5, 271–279.

Alcorn Mackay, S. (2010) *Identifying Trends and Supports for Students with Autism Spectrum Disorder Transitioning into Postsecondary.* Higher Education Quality Council of Ontario. Available at www.heqco.ca/SiteCollectionDocuments/ ASD.pdf, accessed 23 September 2015.

American Psychiatric Association (2000) *Diagnostic and Statistical Manual of Mental Disorders, Fourth Edition.* Washington: American Psychiatric Publishing.

American Psychiatric Association (2013) *Diagnostic and Statistical Manual of Mental Disorders, Fifth Edition.* Arlington: American Psychiatric Association.

Anderson, A. and Wheldall, K. (2004) 'The who, what, where, when, and why of self-monitoring of student behavior.' *Australasian Journal of Special Education 28,* 2, 30–64.

Anderson, L.W., Krathwohl, D.R. and Bloom, B.S. (2001) *A Taxonomy for Learning, Teaching, and Assessing: A Revision of Bloom's Taxonomy of Educational Objectives.* London: Longman.

Antshel, K.M., Zhang-James, Y. and Faraone, S.V. (2013) 'The comorbidity of ADHD and autism spectrum disorder.' *Expert Reviews in Neurotherapy 13,* 10, 1117–1128.

Armstrong, T. (2010) *Neurodiversity: Discovering the Extraordinary Gifts of Autism, ADHD, Dyslexia, and Other Brain Differences.* Philadelphia: De Capo Press.

Attwood, T. (1998). *The Complete Guide to Asperger's Syndrome.* London: Jessica Kingsley Publishers.

Attwood, T. (2006) 'The Patterns and Abilities and Development of Girls with Asperger's Syndrome.' In T. Attwood, T. Grandin, C. Faherty *et al.* (eds) *Asperger's and Girls* (pp. 1–8). Arlington: Future Horizons.

Attwood, T. (2007) *The Complete Guide to Asperger's Syndrome.* London: Jessica Kingsley Publishers.

Australian Federal Government (1992) *Disability Discrimination Act. Australian Federal Government.* Retrieved from www.austlii.edu.au/au/legis/cth/consol_act/dda1992264/, accessed on 10 December 2015.

Autism Spectrum Australia (ASPECT) (2013) *We Belong Study.* Sydney: Autism Spectrum Australia.

Baker-Ward, L., Hess, T.M. and Flannagan, D.A. (1990) 'The effects of involvement on children's memory for events.' *Cognitive Development 5*, 1, 55–69.

Ballard, B. and Clanchy, J. (1991) *Teaching Students from Overseas.* Melbourne: Longman Cheshire.

Bandura, A. (1977) *Social Learning Theory.* Englewood Cliffs: Prentice Hall.

Barnhill, G., Hagiwara, T., Myles, B.S. and Simpson, R. (2000) 'Asperger syndrome: a study of the cognitive profiles of 37 children and adolescents.' *Focus on Autism and Other Developmental Disabilities 15*, 3, 146–153.

Baron-Cohen, S. (1995) *Mindblindness: An Essay in Autism and Theory of Mind.* Cambridge, Massuchusetts: MIT Press.

Baron-Cohen, S. and Wheelwright, S. (2004) 'The empathy quotient: an investigation of adults with Asperger syndrome or high functioning autism, and normal sex differences.' *Journal of Autism and Developmental Disorders 34*, 2, 163–175.

Bellini, S., Akullian, J. and Hopf, A. (2007) 'Increasing social engagement in young children with autism spectrum disorders using video self-monitoring.' *School Psychology Review 36*, 1, 80–90.

Bolick, T. (2006) 'The Launch: Negotiating the Transition from High School to the Great Beyond.' In T. Attwood, T. Grandin, C. Faherty *et al.* (eds) *Asperger's and Girls* (pp. 79–88). Arlington: Future Horizons.

Bowler, D. (1992) '"Theory of Mind" in Asperger Syndrome.' *Journal of Child Psychology 33*, 5, 877–893.

Bradshaw, S. (2013) *Asperger's Syndrome – That Explains Everything: Strategies for Education, Life and Just About Everything Else.* London and Philadelphia: Jessica Kingsley Publishers.

Callahan, K. and Rademacher, J.A. (1999) 'Using self-management strategies to increase the on-task behavior of a student with autism.' *Journal of Positive Behavior Interventions 1*, 2, 117–122.

Cambourne, B. and Turbill, J. (1987) *Coping With Chaos.* Rozelle: Primary English Teachers' Association.

Campbell, A. and Anderson, C.M. (2011) 'Check-In/Check-Out: a systematic evaluation and component analysis.' *Journal of Applied Behavior Analysis 44*, 2, 315–326.

Carrington, S. and Graham, L. (2001) 'Perceptions of school by two teenage boys with Asperger syndrome and their mothers: a qualitative study.' *Autism 5*, 1, 37–48.

Carrington, S., Papinczak, T. and Templeton, E. (2003) 'A phenomenological study: the social world of five adolescents who have Asperger's syndrome.' *Australian Journal of Learning Disabilities 8*, 3, 15–20.

Cash, A.B. (1999) 'A profile of gifted individuals with autism: the twice-exceptional learner.' *Roeper Review 22*, 1, 22–28.

Cleary, T.J. and Zimmerman, B.J. (2004) 'Self-regulation empowerment program: a school-based program to enhance self-regulated and self-motivated cycles of student learning.' *Psychology in the Schools 4*, 1, 537–550.

Cohen, L. and Spenciner, L. (2011) *Assessment of Children and Youth with Special Needs.* Upper Saddle River: Pearson Educational.

Cottrell, S. (2003) *The Study Skills Handbook.* New York: Palgrave Study Guides.

Cumine, V., Leach, J. and Stevenson, G. (1998) *Asperger Syndrome: A Practical Guide for Teachers.* London: David Fulton Publishers.

Cumming, T.M., Strnadova, I. and Singh, S. (2014) 'iPads as instructional tools to enhance learning opportunities for students with developmental disabilities: an action research project.' *Action Research 12*, 2, 151–176.

Davies, M. (2014) 'Secondary School Inclusion and Transition to Life After School.' In P. Foreman and M. Arthur-Kelly (eds) *Inclusion in Action* (pp. 501–550). South Melbourne: Cengage.

Dell, A.G., Newton, D.A. and Petroff, J.G. (2012) *Assistive Technology in the Classroom: Enhancing the Experiences of Students with Disabilities.* Upper Saddle River: Pearson Educational.

Dente, C.L. and Parkinson, K. (2012) 'Ecological approaches to transition planning for students with autism and Asperger's syndrome.' *Children and Schools 34*, 1, 27–36.

Disability Discrimination Act (1992) Canberra: Australian Federal Government. Available at www.austlii.edu.au/au/legis/cth/consol_act/dda1992264, accessed on 10 December 2015.

Disability Standards for Education (2005) Canberra: DEEWR, Australian Federal Government. Available at https://education.gov.au/disability-standards-education, accessed on 10 December 2015.

Dixon, R.M. and Tanner, K. (2013, July) 'The experience of transitioning two adolescents with Asperger syndrome in academically focused high schools.' *Australasian Journal of Special Education 37*, 1, 28–48.

Doige, N. (2007) *The Brain that Changes Itself.* New York: Viking Press.

Draper Rodriguez, C., Strnadova, I. and Cumming, T. (2013) 'Using iPads with students with disabilities: lessons learned from students, teachers and parents.' *Technology Trends 49*, 4, 244-250.

Eagleman, D. (2011) *Incognito: The Secret Lives of the Brain.* New York: Pantheon Books.

Eckes, S. and Ochoa, T.A. (2005) 'Students with disabilities: transitioning from high school to higher education.' *American Secondary Education 33*, 3, 6–20.

Engelkamp, J. (1998) *Memory for Actions.* Hove: Psychology Press.

Farrell, D. and McDougall, D. (2008) 'Self-monitoring of pace to improve math fluency of high school students with disabilities.' *Behavior Analysis International 1*, 2, 26–35.

Finn, L., Ramasay, R., Dukes, C. and Scott, J. (2015) 'Using WatchMinder to increase the on-task behavior of students with autism spectrum disorder.' *Journal of Autism and Other Developmental Disorders 45*, 1408–1418.

Flavell, J.H. (2000) 'Development of children's knowledge about the mental world.' *International Journal of Behavioral Development 24*, 15–23.

Foley-Nipcon, M., Assouline, S. and Stinson, R. (2012) 'Cognitive and academic distinctions between gifted students with autism and Asperger's syndrome.' *Gifted Child Quarterly 33*, 19, 77–89.

Foreman, P. and Arthur-Kelly, M. (2014) *Inclusion in Action.* Melbourne: Cengage.

Foucault, M.T. (1977) *Discipline and Punish: The Birth of the Prison (Translation of: Surveiller et punir; naissance de la prison).* New York: Vintage.

Freedman, S. (2010) *Developing College Skills in Students with Autism and Asperger's Syndrome.* London and Philadelphia: Jessica Kingsley Publishers.

Frith, U. (1989) *Autism: Explaining the Enigma.* Oxford: Blackwell.

Frith, U. (2001) 'Mind blindness and the brain in autism.' *Neuron 32*, 6, 969–979.

Frith, U. and Happé, F. (1994) 'Autism: beyond "Theory of Mind".' *Cognition 50*, 115–132.

Gallimore, R. and Tharp, R. (1990) 'Teaching Mind and Society: Teaching, Schooling, and Literate Discourse.' In L. Moll (ed) *Vygotsky and Education* (pp. 175–205). Cambridge: Cambridge University Press.

Ganz, J.B., Heath, A.K., Davis, J.L. and Vannest, K.L. (2013) 'Effects of a self-monitoring device on socially relevant behaviors in adolescents with Asperger disorder: a pilot study.' *Assistive Technology 25*, 3, 149–157.

Gardner, H. (1993). *Frames of Mind: The Theory of Multiple Intelligences.* New York: Basic Books.

Gardner, H. (1999). *Intelligence Reframed: Multiple Intelligences for the Twenty-First Century.* New York: Basic Books.

Garrison-Wade, D. and Lehmann, J.P. (2009) 'A conceptual framework for understanding students with disabilities' transition to community college.' *Community College Journal of Research and Practice 33*, 5, 415–443.

Gaus, V.L. (2011) 'Cognitive behavioural therapy for adults with autism spectrum disorder.' *Advances in Mental Health and Intellectual Disabilities 5*, 5, 15–25.

Gawrilow, C., Gollwitzer, P.M. and Oettingen, G. (2011) 'If-then plans benefit executive functions in children with ADHD.' *Journal of Social and Clinical Psychology 30*, 6, 616–646.

George Washington University School of Education and Human Development (n.d.) *Students with Autism in the College Classroom.* National Youth Transitions Centre. Available at http://heath.gwu.edu/about-heath, accessed on 22 September 2015.

Gerhart, P.F. and Holmes, D. (2005) 'Employment: Options and Issues for Adolescents and Adults with Autism.' In F. Volkmar, R. Paul, A. Klin and D. Cohen (eds) *Handbook of Autism and Pervasive Developmental Disorders* (pp. 1087–1101). New York: Wiley.

Glennon, T.J. (2001) 'The stress of the university experience for students with Asperger syndrome.' *Work: A Journal of Prevention, Assessment and Rehabilitation 17*, 183–190.

Gluck, R. and Draisma, K. (1997) *The Pipeline Project: An Investigation of Local Infrastructures to Educate Aboriginal Professionals for Community, Professional and Industrial Organisations in the Illawarra and Surrounding Regions.* Canberra: Commonwealth of Australia: Department of Employment, Education, Training and Youth Affairs, Higher Education Division.

Golan, O. and Baron-Cohen, S. (2006) 'Systematizing empathy: Teaching adults with Asperger syndrome or high-functioning autism to recognize complex emotions using interactive media.' *Development and Psychopathology 18*, 591–617.

Gordon, M.L. (2002) 'ADA-based accommodations in higher education: a survey of clinicians about documentation requirements and diagnostic standards.' *Journal of Learning Disabilities 35*, 357–363.

Government of Victoria. (n.d.) *Essay Question Types.* Learning Skills. Available at http://ergo.slv.vic.gov.au/learn-skills/essay-writing-skills/essay-question/types-questions, accessed on 10 December 2015.

Grainger, C., Williams, D.M. and Lind, S.E. (2014a) 'Metacognition, metamemory, and mind-reading in high-functioning adults with autism spectrum disorder.' *Journal of Abnormal Psychology 123*, 3, 650–659.

Grainger, C.E., Williams, D.M. and Lind, S.E. (2014b) 'Online action monitoring and memory for self-performed actions in autism spectrum disorder.' *Journal of Autism and Other Developmental Disorders 44*, 1193–1206.

Grandin, T. (2008) *The Importance of Practical Problem-Solving Skills.* Autism Asperger's Digest. Available at http://autismdigest.com/the-importance-of-practical-problem-solving-skills-2, accessed on 12 December 2015.

Grandin, T. (2013) 'How People with Autism Think.' In E. Schopler and G.B. Mesibov (eds) *Learning and Cognition in Autism* (pp. 137–156). New York and Philadelphia: Springer Science and Business Media.

Hall, T. and Stahl, S. (2006) 'Using Universal Design for Learning to Expand Access to Higher Education.' In M. Adams and S. Brown (eds) *Towards Inclusive Learning in Higher Education* (pp. 67–78). London and New York: Routledge.

Happé, F. and Frith, U. (2006) 'The weak coherence account: detail-focused cognitive style in autism spectrum disorders.' *Journal of Autism and Developmental Disorders* 36, 1, 5–25.

Harpur, J., Lawlor, M. and Fitzgerald, M. (2004) *Succeeding in College with Asperger Syndrome: A Student Guide.* London and Philadelphia: Jessica Kingsley Publishers.

Hatswell, J., Harding, J., Martin, N. and Baron-Cohen, S. (2013, June) *Asperger Syndrome Student Project 2009-12: Final Report.* University of Cambridge Disability Resource Centre. Available at www.disability.admin.cam.ac.uk/files/asprojectreport2013.pdf, accessed on 23 September 2015.

Hattie, J. and Timperley, H. (2007) 'The power of feedback.' *Review of Educational Research* 77, 1, 81–112.

Hawken, L.S. and Horner, R.H. (2003) 'Evaluation of a targeted intervention within a schoolwide system of behaviour support.' *Journal of Behavioral Education* 12, 3, 225–240.

Healey, M., Bradley, A., Fuller, M. and Hall, T. (2006) 'Listening to Students: the Experience of Disabled Students of Learning at University.' In M. Adams and S. Brown (eds) *Towards Inclusive Learning in Higher Education: Developing Curricula for Disabled Students* (pp. 32–43). London and New York: Routledge.

Henderson, H.A., Ono, K.E., McMahon, C.M., Schwartz, C.B., Usher, L.V. and Mundy, P.C. (2015) 'The costs and benefits of self-monitoring for higher functioning children and adolescents with autism.' *Journal of Autism and Other Developmental Disorders* 45, 2, 548–559.

Herera, S. (2005, February 25) *Mildest Autism has 'Selective Advantages'.* NBC News Business. Available at http://www.nbcnews.com/id/7030731/ns/business/t/mild-autismhas-selective-advantages, accessed on 22 July 2014.

Hewitt, L.E. (2011) 'Perspectives on support needs of individuals with autism spectrum disorders: transition to college.' *Topics in Language Disorders* 31, 3, 273–285.

Holifield, C., Goodman, J., Hazelkorn, M. and Heflin, L.J. (2010) 'Using self-monitoring to increase attending to task and academic accuracy in children with autism.' *Focus on Autism and Other Developmental Disabilities* 25, 4, 230–238.

Holliday Willey, L. (1999) *Pretending to be Normal: Living with Asperger's Syndrome.* London: Jessica Kingsley Publishers.

Hurlbert, R., Happé, F. and Frith, U. (1994) 'Sampling the form of inner experience in 3 adults with Asperger Syndrome.' *Psychological Medicine* 24, 2, 385–395.

Huttenlocher, P. (1984) 'Synaptic elimination in the cerebral cortex.' *American Journal of Mental Deficiency* 88, 488–496.

King, M.L. (2011) *Effectiveness of the iPad in Enhancing the Mand Repertoire for Children with Autism. Master of Education Thesis.* Carbondale: Southern Illinois University.

King, M.L., Takeguchi, K., Barry, S.E., Rehfeldt, R.A., Boyer, V.E. and Mathews, T.L. (2014) 'Evaluation of the iPad in the acquisition of requesting skills for children with autism spectrum disorder.' *Research in Autism Spectrum Disorders* 8, 1107–1120.

King-Sears, M.E., Swanson, C. and Mainzer, L. (2011, May) 'TECHnology and literacy for adolescents with disabilities.' *Journal of Adolescent and Adult Literacy 54*, 8, 569–578.

Kuder, S.J. (2013) *Teaching Students with Language and Communication Disabilities.* Upper Saddle River: Pearson Educational.

Langford, P.E. (2005) *Vygotsky's Developmental and Educational Psychology.* Hove and New York: Psychology Press.

Lavoie, R. (1989) *How Difficult Can This Be? FAT City – A Learning Disabilities Workshop.* Barnstable: WETA/PBS.

Legge, B.D., DeBar, R.M. and Alber-Morgan, S.R. (2010) 'The effects of self-monitoring with a Motivaider on the on-task behavior of fifth and sixth graders with autism and other disabilities.' *Journal of Behavior Assessment and Intervention in Children 1*, 1, 43–52.

Light, J. and McNaughton, D. (2013) 'Putting people first: re-thinking the role of technology in augmentative and alternative communication intervention.' *International Society for Augmentative and Alternative Communication 29*, 4, 299–309.

Lijfft, M., Kenemans, J., Verbaten, M. and van Engeland, H. (2005) 'A meta-analytic review of stopping performance in ADHD: deficient inhibitory motor control?' *Journal of Abnormal Psychology 114*, 216–222.

Locke, J., Kasari, C. and Wood, J.J. (2014) 'Assessing social skills in early-aged children with autism spectrum disorders: the Social Skills Q-Sort.' *Journal of Psychological Assessment 32*, 1.

Loftin, R.L., Gibb, A.C. and Skiba, R. (2005) 'Using self-monitoring strategies to address behavior and academic issues.' *Impact 18*, 2, 12–13.

Lopez, B., Leekam, S.R. and Arts, G.R. (2008) 'How central is central coherence? Preliminary evidence on the link between conceptual and perceptual processing in children with autism.' *Autism 12*, 2, 159–171.

March, R.E. and Horner, R.H. (2002) 'Feasibility and contributions of functional behavioral assessment in schools.' *Journal of Emotional and Behavioral Disorders 10*, 3, 158–170.

Martin, R. (2011) *Top Tips for Asperger Students: How to Get the Most out of University or College.* London and Philadelphia: Jessica Kingsley Publishers.

Martino McCarty, M. (2012) *The Experience of College Students Diagnosed with Asperger's Disorder and Participating in a University-Based Autism Spectrum Disorder Transitional Support Program.* Ed D Thesis. Margaret Warner Graduate School of Education and Human Development, University of Rochester.

McMahon-Coleman, K. (2013) *Teaching Sheldon: Autism on TV and in the Classroom.* PopCAANZ Conference. Brisbane.

McMahon-Coleman, K. (2015) *Why Doc Martin Hates Being Called Doc Martin: Autism Spectrum Disorder on TV.* Wellington: PopCAANZ.

Merzenich, M. (2013) *Soft-Wired: How the New Science of Brain Plasticity Can Change Your Life.* San Francisco: Parnassus Publishing.

Minshew, N., Goldstein, G. and Siegel, D.J. (1997) 'Neuropsychologic functioning in autism: profile of a complex information processing disorder.' *Journal of the International Neuropsychological Society 3*, 4, 303–316.

Mottron, J. and Belleville, S. (1993) 'A study of perceptual analysis in a high-level autistic subject with exceptional graphic abilities.' *Brain and Cognition 23*, 2, 279–309.

Murza, K.A. and Nye, C. (2013) 'Pragmatic language intervention for adults with Asperger syndrome or high-functioning autism: a feasibility study.' *Contemporary Issues in Communication and Science Disorders 40*, 85–97.

Neuman, D., Spezio, M., Piven, J. and Adolphs, R. (2006) 'Looking you in the mouth: abnormal gaze in autism resulting from impaired top-down modulation of visual attention.' *Social Cognitive and Affective Neuroscience 1*, 3, 194–202.

Newland, B. (2003) 'Evaluating the Impact of a VLE on Learning and Teaching.' *Proceedings of the EDMEDIA World Conference on Educational Multimedia, Hypermedia and Telecommunications* (pp. 601–603). Chesapeake: AACE.

Newland, B., Boyd, V. and Pavey, J. (2006) 'Enhancing Disabled Students' Learning through Virtual Learning Environments.' In M. Adams and S. Brown (eds) *Towards Inclusive Learning in Higher Education: Developing Curricula for Disabled Students* (pp. 143–153). London and New York: Routledge.

Norris, N. (2014) *A New Perspective on Thinking, Memory and Learning in Gifted Adults with Asperger Syndrome: Five Phenomenological Case Studies (PhD thesis).* Wollongong: University of Wollongong. Available at http://ro.uow.edu.au/theses/4242, accessed on 10 December 2015.

Palmer, A. (2006) *Realizing the College Dream with Autism or Asperger Syndrome: A Parent's Guide to Student Success.* London and Philadelphia: Jessica Kingsley Publishers.

Pearson, E. and Koppi, T. (2006) 'Supporting Staff in Developing Inclusive Online Learning.' In M. Adams and S. Brown (eds) *Towards Inclusive Learning in Higher Education: Developing Curricula for Disabled Students* (pp. 56–66). London and New York: Routledge.

Pennington, R.C. and Delano, M.E. (2012) 'Writing instruction for students with autism spectrum disorder: a review of literature.' *Focus on Autism and Other Developmental Disabilities 27*, 3, 158–167.

Perner, L. (2002a) *If I'd Known Then What I Know Now: What I Have Learned About Life with Asperger's Syndrome, and What Still Eludes Me.* Autism, Asperger's Syndrome and the Autism Spectrum. Available at www.autism-help.org/story-adult-know-now.htm, accessed on 22 July 2014.

Perner, L. (2002b) *Preparing to Be Nerdy Where Nerdy Can Be Cool: College Planning for Students on the Autism Spectrum.* Online Conference Proceedings. Indianapolis, IN: Autism Society of America. Available at www.autismspectrum.org.au/sites/default/files/Vic/Preparing%20for%20College.pdf, accessed on 10 March 2016.

Perner, J., Frith, U., Leslie, A. and Leekam, S. (1989) 'Exploration of the autistic child's theory of mind: knowledge, belief and communication.' *Child Development 60*, 3, 689–700.

Riffel, L.A. (2008) *Interventions for Children with Attention Deficit Hyperactivity Disorder, Attention Deficit Disorder.* EDST 5107 Moodle. Available at http://moodle.telt.unsw.edu.au/mod/book/view.php?id=540900andchapterid=77725, accessed on 21 May 2015.

Robillard, M., Mayer-Crittenden, M., Roy-Charland, A., Minor-Corriveau, M. and Belanger, R. (2013) 'Exploring the impact of cognition on young children's ability to navigate a speech-generating device.' *Augmentative and Alternative Communication 29*, 4, 347–359.

Sadock, B. and Sadock, V.A. (2007) *Kaplan and Sadock's Synopsis of Psychiatry: Behavioral Sciences/Clinical Psychiatry* (tenth ed.). Philadelphia: Wolers Kluwer: Lippincott Williams and Wilkins.

Sansosti, F.J. and Powell-Smith, K.A. (2010) *High-Functioning Autism/Asperger Syndrome in Schools: Assessment and Intervention.* New York: Guilford Press.

Schon, D. (1983) *The Reflective Practitioner.* New York: Basic Books.

Sciutto, M., Richwine, S., Mentrikoski, J. and Niedzwiecki, K. (2012) 'A qualitative analysis of the school experiences of students with Asperger syndrome.' *Focus on Autism and Other Developmental Disabilities 27*, 3, 177–188.

Servilio, K.L. and Mazzone, T. (2012) 'What's happening: app promotes communications.' *The Exceptional Parent 42*, 10, 6–7.

Simone, R. (2010) *Aspergirls: Empowering Females with Asperger's Syndrome.* Philadelphia: Jessica Kingsley Publishers.

Skuse, D. (2012) 'DSM-5's conceptualization of autistic disorders.' *Journal of the American Academy of Child and Adolescent Psychiatry 51*, 4, 343–346.

Soares, D.A., Vannest, K.J. and Harrison, J. (2009) 'Computer aided self-monitoring to increase academic production and reduce self-injurious behavior in a child with autism.' *Behavioral Interventions 24*, 3, 171–183.

Sodian, B. and Frith, U. (2008) 'Metacognition, Theory of Mind, and self-control: the relevance of high-level cognitive processes in development, neuroscience, and education.' *Mind, Brain and Education 2*, 3, 111–113.

Stanovich, P. and Jordan, A. (2000) 'Effective teaching as effective intervention.' *Learning Disabilities 10*, 4, 235–238.

Stasolla, F., Perilli, V. and Daniani, R. (2014) 'Self-monitoring to promote on-task behaviour by two high functioning boys with ASD and symptoms of ADHD.' *Research in Autism Spectrum Disorders 8*, 5, 472–479.

Strnadova, I. and Cumming, T.M. (2016) *Lifespan Transitions and Disability: A Holistic Perspective.* New York: Routledge.

Suciu, M. (2014) 'UNE mentoring program for students living with autism spectrum disorders (ASDs).' *Journal of the Australia and New Zealand Student Services Association,* 55–59.

Tantam, D. (2003) 'Assessment and Control of Comorbid Emotional and Behaviour Problems.' In M. Prior (ed.) *Learning and Behavior Problems in Asperger Syndrome* (pp. 148–174). New York: The Guilford Press.

Tantam, D., Holmes, D. and Cordess, C. (1993) 'Nonverbal expression in autism of Asperger type.' *Journal of Autism and Developmental Disorders 23*, 1, 111–133.

Trent Bruce, N. (2014, July) *A Qualitative Case Study Investigating the Graduation and Job Placement Outcomes of College Student with Autism Spectrum Disorder: Implications for Higher Education Leaders.* Ed D Thesis.

Tulving, E. (2002) 'Episodic memory: from mind to brain.' *Annual Review of Psychology 53*, 1, 1–25.

UNESCO (1994) *The Salamanca Statement and Framework for Action on Special Needs Education.* Salamanca, Spain: UNESCO.

United Nations (UN) General Assembly (1989) *Convention on the Rights of the Child.* United Nations. Retrieved from Office of the Human Rights High Commissioner, available at www.ohchr.org/en/professionalinterest/pages/crc.aspx, accessed on 10 March 2016.

vanBergeijk, E., Klin, A. and Volkmar, F. (2008) 'Supporting more able students on the autism spectrum: college and beyond.' *Journal of Autism and Developmental Disorders 38*, 1359–1370.

Vygotsky, L.S., Cole, M., John-Steiner, V., Scribner, S. and Souberman, E. (1978) *Mind in Society: The Development of Higher Psychological Processes.* Cambridge: Harvard University Press.

Wagner, S. (2002) *Inclusive Programming for Middle School Students with Autism/Asperger's Syndrome.* Arlington: Future Horizons.

Wagner, S. (2009) *Inclusive Programming for High School Students with Autism or Asperger's Syndrome.* Arlington: Future Horizons.

Wearing, C. (2010) 'Autism, metaphor and relevance theory.' *Mind and Language 25*, 2, 196–216.

Wenzel, C. and Rowley, L. (2010, May/June) 'Teaching social skills and academic strategies to college students with Asperger's syndrome.' *Teaching Exceptional Children 42*, 5, 44–50.

Wertsch, J. (1978) 'Adult-child interaction and the roots of metacognition.' *Quarterly Newsletter of the Institute for Comparative Human Development 1*, 15–18.

Williams, D. and Happé, F. (2009) 'Pre-conceptual aspects of self-awareness in autism spectrum disorder: the case of action monitoring.' *Journal of Autism and Developmental Disorders 39*, 251–259.

Williams, D. and Happé, F. (2010) 'Representing intentions in self and other: studies of autism and typical development.' *Developmental Science 13*, 2, 307–319.

Williams, E. (2004) 'Who really needs a "theory" of mind?: an interpretive phenomenological analysis of the autobiographical writings of ten high-functioning individuals with an autism spectrum disorder.' *Theory and Psychology 14*, 5, 704–724.

Williams, J.G., Allison, C., Scott, F.J., Bolton, P.F., Baron-Cohen, S., Matthews, F.E. and Brayne, C. (2008) 'The Childhood Autism Spectrum Disorder Test (CAST): sex differences.' *Journal of Autism and Developmental Disorders 38*, 1731–1739.

Wolf, L.E., Thierfeld Brown, J. and Kukiela Bork, G.R. (2009) *Students with Asperger Syndrome: A Guide for College Personnel.* Shawnee Mission: Autism Asperger Publishing Company.

Wright, J. (2013) *How To: Teach Students to Change Behaviors Through Self-Monitoring.* Intervention Central. Available at www.interventioncentral.org/node/961544, accessed on 11 December 2015.

Yoshida, Y. (2012) *Raising Children with Asperger's Syndrome and High-Functioning Autism: Championing the Individual.* London and Philadelphia: Jessica Kingsley Publishers.

# Subject Index

# Author Index

CPSIA information can be obtained
at www.ICGtesting.com
Printed in the USA
FFOW01n2033080616
24740FF